WHAT THE CF

"Colleen Rae teaches writing from the inside out, which is the only way to teach it properly. This is an invaluable book."

—*Julia Cameron, Author,* The Artist's Way

"If you're the sort of reader who starts at the back of a book, you're in for a real treat. The bibliography is excellent. But be sure and begin at the beginning, too. By means of simple exercises and with minimal fuss, Colleen Rae leads a prospective fiction writer through the process moving from vignette to short story. Secret keys to a Magic Kingdom, like characterization, point of view, conflict resolution and voice, are here and accessible. And you'll find, reading through, that the mysteries of writing fiction aren't so mysterious after all."

—*Sage Walker, Novelist and short story writer. Her short fiction has appeared in* Asimov's *magazine, in "An Armory of Swords", edited by Fred Saberhagen; and in "Marked Cards" and "Black Trump",* Wild Cards *series edited by George R. R. Martin. Her new novel* Whiteout, *is published by Tor Books.*

"I'm not a devotee of writers' manuals, but I make an exception for Colleen Rae's *Movies in the Mind.* The reason is that this manual is a real book, and the reason for that, I believe, is that every sentence is filled with personality. This personality— a sympathetic, interesting, sometimes baffled, almost always sensible one—is Colleen Rae herself. She *wants to help you write fiction,* so much that there is a very good chance she will help *you.*"

—*Richard Stern, Novelist, short story writer, essayist. His most recent books are* A Sistermony *(Heartland Award 1995);* One Person and Another; Noble Rot Stories *1949-88 and* Shares and Other Fictions. *He is Regenstein Professor of English, University of Chicago.*

"As a creative writing teacher I have looked at numerous creative writing texts most of which separate chapters by character, plot etc. essentially isolating each element of fiction and creating the impression that writers may "dip in" to the text at any point. Colleen Rae's *Movies in the Mind* book, however, emphasizes that creative writing can and should follow some sort of process and writing is hard work—something that must be done everyday. I am also quite impressed at the writing activities that accompany each chapter—they effectively supplement the chapter discussions, and they sound most interesting; in fact, I am eager to test them out myself."

—*Linda Poziwilko, Department of Literature, Belmont University, Nashville*

MOVIES
IN THE MIND

How to Build a Short Story

COLLEEN MARIAH RAE

SHERMAN ASHER Publishing

Acknowledgments

Parts of Chapter Five first appeared as "Tools for Creating Emotionally Powerful Fiction" in the 1994 *Writer's Digest Novel and Short Story Market*

First Edition
ISBN 0-9644196-5-3

Library of Congress Cataloging-in-Publication Data

Rae , Colleen Mariah.
 Movies in the mind : how to build a short story / Colleen Mariah Rae . — 1st ed .
  p. cm.
 Includes bibliographical references and index.
 ISBN 0-9644196-5-3
 1. Short story. 2. Fiction — Authorship.   I. Title.
PN3373.R29 1996
808.3′1--dc20   96-21304
                                                       CIP

Printed in the USA on acid free paper
Book design by Judith Rafaela
Cover Design by Joanne Yanoff
Front cover photograph by Richard Alan Ries
Back cover photograph by Gil Asher

Sherman Asher Publishing
PO Box 2853
Santa Fe, NM, 87504

ACKNOWLEDGMENTS

I want to thank the many students I have had over the years—at writers conferences and in classes, workshops, and seminars—who have helped me shape the material in this book. However, the ones to whom I owe the greatest debt are Ruth Barks, Ron Barks, Bea Bragg, Jonathan Briggs, Eloisa Bergere Brown, Lynn Butler, Sucha Cardoza, Patricia Carey, Mitch Cullin, Marion Davidson, Carley Dawson, Harriett Faudree Dublin, Rob Earle, Stephanie Farrow, Richard Fleming, Penny Hansen, Michael Hice, Marigay Graña, Pat Hinnebusch, Michele Lommasson, Kathleen Keenan, Sherry King, Deanna Kirby, Joan Mason, Marvin Mattis, Naomi Mattis, Jim McBride, Altina Miranda, Luis Molinar, David Oberdorfer, Danny O'Neil, Avrum Organick, Rebecca Saunders, Leda Silver, Judith Sherman Asher, Rose Mary Stearns, John Talley, Sherry Weinstein, and Nedra Westwater.

Special thanks go to my star student, Rick Ferber, aka Richard Goldstein, whose unflagging determination to succeed as a writer has given me some of my greatest satisfaction as a teacher.

I also want to thank Ruth Barks for her loving editing of this manuscript; my publisher Judith Sherman Asher for her dedication to making this the best book it could possibly be; David Sontag for his encouragement and support; Ruth Crowley, Catherine Garland, Phyllis Hotch, Phil Wyant, as well as many others, for sponsoring my workshops; Jack Heffron for being a pal on this sometimes dry and dusty road of writing; and last but certainly not least, my mentor Richard Stern, head of the creative writing program at the University of Chicago, for his belief in me that set me firmly on this path.

Colleen Mariah Rae
Santa Fe, New Mexico
April 1996

To Dr. Reina Attias
who gave me back my life

TABLE OF CONTENTS

PREFACE   1

ENTERING THE STORYMAKER'S REALM   5

FICTION'S BUILDING BLOCKS   11

PARTICIPATORY ART   24

DIGGING THE CLAY   39

WHOSE STORY IS IT ANYWAY?   70

UNLOCKING YOUR STORY   79

HOW TO BIRTH A STORY   102

THERE'S ALWAYS A CRITIC   116

EXERCISE PAGES   128

READING LIST   134

INDEX   137

PREFACE

In the fall of 1987, I got what I've since referred to as "My National Endowment for the Arts Grant" — I was fired twice in thirty-two days and ended up on unemployment. During that period, I managed to turn a big lemon into lemonade: in between searching for a job and writing free-lance columns and articles to supplement the pittance unemployment pays, I wrote fiction. And although I already had an M.A. in creative writing and had been writing fiction in my spare time for seven years, I decided to come at it as a rank beginner, using every how-to book and every interview with an author I could get my hands on. Also, on a daily basis I kept a record of my writing process. I was, as I wrote in my journal, "trying to shape my technique so that when this year of incredible fertility passes, I'll be able to produce because I'll know how to tap the material."

It worked. Not only did I write twelve short stories and a short novel in fourteen months, but I'd shaped my technique and had found ways to short circuit the fiction-writing process. In 1989, I began teaching others how to do it, too, in my *How to Build a Short Story* classes in the adult education program at Santa Fe Community College. That course became a workshop that I taught around the country, and it also grew into a follow-up course I called *The Craft of Fiction*. When students from *Craft* wanted to continue I developed *The Storyteller's Voice*, and that led to *The Master's Craft: Breaking all the Rules*. Finally, because so many of my students were having, as I'd had, a story refuse to be short, I developed *The Keys to Dramatic Structure* to show a way to approach novels with some idea of the lay of the land. Then sex reared its head: I developed *Writing Between the Sheets* to help my students create better love scenes.

As I taught my classes, talked at writers conferences, and gave workshops around the country, students' questions led me to more breakthroughs; I found better ways of presenting material so it made more sense, was easier to use, led to better results.

All of those classes, workshops, and conference lectures led to a series of books. This one is the kickoff in the *Movies in the Mind* lineup. The others follow the sequence of my classes: *The Craft of Fiction; The Storyteller's Voice; The Master's Craft: Breaking all the Rules; The Keys to Dramatic Structure;* and *Writing Between the Sheets.*

Now about this book: Most writing techniques approach fiction from a product orientation. This book teaches you *process,* and although there are other books on process, this one does what they don't do: it leads to a product. It's a proven system for producing a short story in a very short time.

This book follows the structure I have used successfully in my *How to Build a Short Story* classes and workshops. I take you step by step through the process of writing so that if you do all the exercises as you come to them, you will have a story well underway by the time you finish the book.

In Chapter One, you will discover how to use *The Movies in the Mind* to partner with your storymaker so its story can be told. And with *The Critic's Page,* you'll begin to make your inner critic an ally in your fiction writing process.

In Chapter Two, I'll be talking about what makes a story good. It's a one word answer: *Images.* They're fiction's building blocks, and without the alchemy of being able to reproduce taste, touch, sight, sound, and smell in the mind's eye of the reader, you can't transport them to your fictional dream. Two exercises are *Nightly Recap* and *Round Robin.*

In Chapter Three, I'll show you how to take images and produce emotionally powerful stories; you'll be working with your brain's limbic system using my technique of *Method Writing* to produce what I call *Participatory Art.*

In Chapter Four, you will find out where stories come from. I'll be using one of my own short stories, "God's Will," to show how a story evolves from *image seed* to finished product through digging the clay. And I give you guidelines for your own clay digging.

In Chapter Five, you'll dig some more clay with my *Dilemma* and *Continuum Trait* techniques and start unearthing *the* story your character *most* wants you to tell.

In Chapter Six, you'll continue the clay digging with *Perspective Trials,* a technique I developed to help you find the right voice for *this* story. You'll learn how to find the right camera angle, point of view, distance in time, audience — all of which give the right perspective for *this* story.

In Chapter Seven, you get to do nothing — and it's harder than it sounds. The *immersion* and *active incubation* techniques I teach you will help overcome "writer's block," which I call "the story's not ready to be birthed." A lot of people who have writer's block are suffering merely from the fact that the unconscious hasn't written the story yet. I will give you ways to help the unconscious get to the point that it can write the story for you in one sitting: My *Silent Movies* technique will help make the labor short and sweet.

In Chapter Eight, you'll learn *The Art of Critique.* Critique is something that needs to be taught; people do not know how to give good feedback to a story, and too often we do what we'd never do when it comes to fixing our car or our psyche — we turn to rank amateurs. Herein lies a warning about writing groups.

EXERCISES

This book is very much a hands-on kind of process: exercises are woven into each chapter that will help move your story along. But remember: nothing comes from nothing. You have to put in the time to get the product. With the first exercises, even fifteen minutes of writing will prime you to partner with your unconscious, to stoke its fires, to give it stuff to work with *if you do it every day.* When it comes to the birth, however, you'll really need to spend the time — a solid block of time — to get results. Until you've had the experience of immersing yourself in the birthing process, you don't know what a joy this can be. Make sure you let yourself have the time to really get into it. Maybe even go away for a day or two so you can write without interruption.

If you put in the time and do all the exercises, I guarantee you that you will be able to write a short story. It won't be a crafted story — that's a whole new set of techniques that I present in the second book in this series, *Movies in the Mind: The Craft of Fiction* — but it'll be a story with a beginning, middle, and end that's ready for you to craft into its most beautiful form.

CHAPTER ONE

ENTERING THE STORYMAKER'S REALM

This is a book about getting out of your own way so that the storymaker inside of you can tell its stories. You've already got the only equipment you'll ever need to do it: your mind's eye — that place inside of you that's like a movie screen, but with a difference. On that "screen," you don't just see and hear as you would with a regular movie, you taste and touch and smell and slip into the bodies of your characters and see the world through their eyes, touch it with their hands, smell it with their noses.

It's like the world of dreams, but not as formless. Movies have a structure that allows the audience — or the reader — to transport themselves into the fictional dream. That's your job as a writer: to create that dream for your reader by *chronicling the movies in the mind*. There's no author intrusion, you're just noting what you see, hear, taste, touch, smell in your mind's eye.

Fortunately, chronicling the *movies in the mind* is not only an easy job, it's one that is great fun. The most magical part about writing fiction — the thing impossible to understand until we experience it — is that stories play themselves out on the screen in our mind with a volition all their own. I've literally fallen out of my chair laughing at the antics of my characters. And that's what's fun about writing fiction — the pure entertainment value of watching the movies in the mind once we learn to get out of our own way and partner with our storymaker.

It's fun, but you must also be prepared. Writers — like all artists — go into an uncharted realm of inner space every time we create. We pull the new into the now. And because we're going to the frontier, it can be a scary process: Rollo May said in *The Courage to Create* that for the creative person, fear never goes away. We learn to go on in the face of it — sometimes even welcoming the fear because it's a sign that we're truly tapping *the well*. The well: that source of inspiration that the ancient Greeks called the Muses and that many of us now call the unconscious. Who knows what the well really is? But it's there to be drawn from by anyone brave enough to go where no one has ever gone before.

For each of us the way to the well is different. That's why every artist must become aware of his or her own *process* and become the mapmaker, naming the terrain so that the way back is known.

In my own naming, I came to see how my writing process wasn't the linear one some writers report. I can't sit down and have the story unfold under my pen. No, my process, I realized, was like that of a sculptor who works first in clay. I start with an incident that has been haunting me, and then I spend a lot of time scribbling in notebooks, *digging the clay* through conversations with my characters, through detailing up scenes, through trial runs with voice, and so on.

From all this clay digging, I get just the right stuff unearthed, including the "wire hanger" that serves as the armature for my story. Then I slap on the best of the clay. Once I get the rough form, I then get to do what I like most of all — shape the story into its most beautiful form.

As you go through this book doing the exercises, you'll realize what your own process is because your way will either be like mine and you'll feel comfortable doing it my way, or it won't feel comfortable and you'll have to start looking at what's going on and how *you* work as a writer. You'll know automatically that my way is not the way for you. And that's what this is about: I'm serving as a guide. If it works for you great; if not, it will help you refine your process just because doing it my way will be a frustrating experience.

As you go along, make a conscious effort to name your own process. Your survival as a writer depends upon it. Naming becomes your map to help you find your way back to these usually imperceptible realms of inner space.

During the storymaker's turn, our goal is to move away from

what I call tip-of-the-iceberg thinking and really become immersed in chronicling the movies in our minds. In fact, our goal is to become so immersed that we lose all track of time because it's then that our story will start telling itself. When that happens, stuff comes up from the well that we look at with awe, thinking, "Where did that come from?" We know that never in a million years could *we* have written *that*. It's too wonderful. It's stuff like Mary La Chapelle wrote in her story "The Gate House." The narrator is a younger woman, who is by the end of the story a schoolteacher at the church school. She tells the story of two older women who call themselves sisters and who live together in the gate house at the cemetery. This is the fifth paragraph from the story's end:

> They hung their laundry out on the deck at night, to keep the messiness of it in the dark, they said. In the early dusk one evening I left the classroom late, in time to catch them just finishing this task. They turned to each other as though they were just finishing a talk between themselves when Connie bent over, her arms curled out before her. I thought at first something was physically wrong, but the way Clara embraced her sister, I realized Connie was crying. I backed into the shadow of the school building and watched. Connie was hidden in Clara's arms with just a small part of her dark head protruding from a corner of Clara's shoulder. My strongest impression was the rhythmic movement of Clara's arm as she patted Connie's back. Over and over she patted her, until I could no longer see them in the resolute darkness, and I shuddered as I walked home with my first comprehension that pain could be constant and rhythmic like that, that the comforter needed to find the rhythm and know it, as Clara must know Connie's.

As the story continues, Clara dies. Four paragraphs later, La Chapelle ends the story with these words:

> I couldn't go to Connie. I was not old enough, nor brave enough. I could not watch over her. All it seemed I could do was just watch her, furtively from the churchyard. Two dusky nights I watched that woman as she wandered over the deck's surface. She fiddled with unnecessary laundry, sometimes stopping to exclaim words to a billowing clean shirt or to ribbons of clean stockings. Sometimes she huddled

over in that hurt way. But I couldn't go to her. I didn't know the rhythm, not yet.

This has all the marks of Mary La Chapelle's having really tapped the well — it takes the breath away with its rightness, with the rhythmic pat of the words "not yet." I can often tell when one of my students hits this place where the story starts telling itself and we're simply recording—Jonathan Briggs did when he was telling the tale of how some high school boys were interrupted while siphoning gas in a funeral home parkng lot. The gas began to overflow the can.

> Just then a man turns the corner from the front of the funeral home. He's in a suit and probably is coming from the wake. He stops and lights a cigarette and heads for the Impala. In the same instant I realize the smell of gasoline is real. A rainbowed puddle of the stuff leaking out from under the front of the Impala. The can is overflowing. The man is walking towards a river of gasoline. The cigarette in his hand trails a cirrus cloud of smoke. I'm frozen in place.
>
> Suddenly something swishes past me. It streaks toward the river of gas and the man. It reaches the man and seems to veer off from him like a billiard ball off the rubber. The man turns to follow it with his eyes and shouts something as he gestures with the hand that has — no — had the cigarette in it. The streak stops a few yards from him and turns into JR. He yells at the man, "Thanks, Mister," and takes a drag on the cigarette. Then he turns and runs away.

When Jonathan read this, the image of this boy swooping down, snatching the cigarette, and yelling, "Thanks, Mister," delighted me. I've come to know that there's a one-to-one correspondence between my experience of awe or delight and the author's success at chronicling. I said to Jonathan, "You really tapped the well when JR grabbed the man's cigarette."

"Yeah," he said. "I watched him do that and nearly cracked up." It especially surprised Jonathan because JR hadn't seemed the kind of character to do something like that — which made it, of course, all the more wonderful.

These are not the sort of things we *think to*; they come flying up unbidden from the well just because we are chronicling the movies in our mind. And that's the fiction writer's task.

But don't take the word "task" too seriously. As Anthony Storr says in *Solitude: A Return to the Self,*

> It seems probable that there is always an element of play in creative living. When this playful element disappears, joy goes with it, and so does any sense of being able to innovate. Creative people not infrequently experience periods of despair in which their ability to create anything new seems to have deserted them. This is often because a particular work has become invested with such overwhelming importance that it is no longer possible to play with it.

In fact, though creative people do suffer bouts of despair, one of the things creativity researchers long ago identified as a trait characteristic of creative people is a sense of humor. As one of my students said, "Creative people seem to laugh more." And that includes laughing at themselves. That's one of the secrets to tapping the well. Make it light; make it play. Never, never, never take it — or yourself as artist — too seriously or the well dries up. If that ever happens to you, the best book I've ever found for getting it flowing again is Julia Cameron's *The Artist's Way* — probably because she knows the power of play!

As soon as you do start playing, though, the tip-of-the iceberg part of the brain starts speaking. This is the schooled part, the part that learned how to do an essay in high school and will tell you about beginnings, middles, and ends. I call this part the critic. What I want you to realize is that your critic is your best ally — if you train it. And training it is something you'll begin to do as you do the exercises in this book.

Before that time, there's only one thing you need to do: honor your critic.

Honor the critic? Exactly.

THE CRITIC'S PAGE

Across the top of a sheet of paper, write THE CRITIC'S PAGE in big, bold letters. This is not a joke; it's probably the most important exercise I'm going to ask you to do. So important that I have provided one on page 128 to start you off.

Every time your critic makes any comment about what you're working on, I want you to write that comment down on The Critic's Page. I also want you to code the page so that you can find it later. For instance, if you're writing longhand in a spiral notebook when your critic says, "That's the worst piece of drivel I've ever heard," put a number next to the thing you'd just written in your notebook and put the same number on your Critic's Page with "That's the worst piece of drivel I've ever heard" next to the number. At the same time you're doing this, I want you to say to your critic, "Thank you for pointing that out. I'll write it down here so I can come back to it when it's your turn. It's not your turn right now; it's the storymaker's turn. But I do appreciate your help."

This sounds corny, but it works because your critic is just like any of us: it only wants to be listened to and heard. And, besides, honoring the critic ends a war that never should have started in the first place because it is absolutely impossible to create without both the storymaker and the critic. So every time your critic speaks, say thanks, record the advice, but remind your critic that you've got to get the material up from the well first or it won't have anything to work with when your storymaker is done.

CHAPTER TWO

FICTION'S BUILDING BLOCKS

What makes a story good? It is not that it's grammatically perfect, not even that it's skillfully rendered. No, sometimes those technical things get in the way of evoking what every writer must evoke in the reader: the dream. What makes a story good is that we can't quite shake it, that it keeps coming back unbeckoned like a dream we once had or a memory of an experience that sifts into consciousness in odd moments. It lives inside of us for months or years. It tangles into the web of our life so inextricably that, yes, it *haunts* us.

There is a reason for that, and it's not the words: it's the images. Images are the most powerful memory device there is. That is why ancient Greeks used images as mnemonics and why memory trainers use images today. For most people, imaging is a powerful memory tool. I had my first taste of this ten years ago when I took imaging techniques taught me by a memory trainer and used them to remember the names of more than eighty of my college students the first day of the fall quarter. For me, this seemed an impossible feat. Yet I did it — I knew everyone's name on the second day of class. No prompting. All it took was seeing Suzy with a big letter *q* sewn on her shirt, the man named Nanak like "Nanook of the North," and Mary wearing a wedding dress. Amazingly it worked, and having always been abysmal at remembering names, I became convinced of the power of images.

It is images that make us remember a storybook read to us as children; we can still taste the cookies and icy cold milk left out for Santa Claus. It is images that trigger the memory of grandma's kitchen when we walk into a house where bread is baking. Just the smell is enough to transport us. It is images that turn a squeak into a body memory of soaring high on a swing. Through the alchemy of image, we can be instantly transported to another place, another time. That is why they are fiction's building blocks. They ignite the dream by letting us hear, taste, touch, see, feel, and smell in our mind's eye.

Read this passage as you would a piece of fiction:

> One summer day, an old Spanish man walked into the small southwestern town library where I worked. He walked with a cane made of a polished and reinforced cactus skeleton. Stooping under the low, adobe-thickened entry way, the smell of his sunbaked sourness pierced the cool room. With each step toward me, his cane struck the flagstone with a pistol clap. His old penny-colored eyes flashed in his corrugated face as he demanded with a soft-spoken, pure Spanish lisp a book on the Mexican War.

Can you see this old man in your mind's eye? Is he clear to you? How about feeling the cool room? What does it do to the hair on the skin of your forearms? Can you stand by the doorway where the sun and the dim of the room meet and feel the admixture of the cool and the hot there? Do you feel the difference on your body between both sides? Can you smell the old man? Is there anything you can taste? And the sound of the cane — hear it? How about his voice? Is it like a whisper or as clear as the voice on a TV? Or do you not hear it at all?

Most of us, when we come across a descriptive passage in a book, do more than just read it. We experience it. We crawl into the world created by the author and live in it as we would in our own — all senses operating. Through the alchemy of images, we see and hear and smell and taste and touch without any direct input from the external world to our senses.

But images do more than keep readers in the dream. They transmit information about the character — oftentimes quite subliminally. What, for instance, do you know about the old man? That he is assertive? I didn't have to tell you that here's somebody who, by God, is going to get what he wants. Before he "demanded," you knew this — even if you didn't consciously know that you knew. And there's a simple reason for this: how can you make a cane have a pistol clap? What sort of a movement do you have to do to give a pistol clap? Just one image — "pistol clap" — told you reams about that man; I could not have achieved that same effect by writing two paragraphs. That's why *an image is worth much, much more than a thousand words.*

Here's an example from the beginning of the Japanese writer Mori Yoko's "Be It Ever So Humble":

> It was slightly past lunchtime in the restaurant. Most of the customers had finished eating and were now sitting cosily behind their cups of coffee.
> Through the window facing the main street the leafless branches of a maple, the image of a tree on a Bernard Buffet canvas, pointed at a cloudy winter sky. Apparently there was wind outside, for its naked twigs shifted uncomfortably in the chill of the afternoon.
> Inside the restaurant, however, it was warm and restful. No music flowed; only the chimes of teaspoons on china accompanied the low melody of female conversation. Vases of bright flowers stood around like colorful islands among aromatic currents of espresso.
> For some time now, Akiko had been gazing at the bare branches outside the window.

Now anthropomorphism is risky; but by saying the tree's "naked twigs shifted uncomfortably," Yoko gave us the character's mood — especially surrounded as it was by the contrast of the restaurant's atmosphere of warmth and color. Yoko could have written that the woman was feeling great discomfort or unease or anxiety, but that wouldn't have left such an unsettled impact on us because it wouldn't have entered our being in the same sort of "from the bottom up" way.

Images like these, that are *worth much more than a thousand words* come from being a good chronicler of the movies in our mind. Notice for instance how a character — call her Sarah — walks across a room. How does Sarah plant her feet on the floor? Toe to heel or heel to toe? Are her feet splayed or do her toes point straight ahead?

Does she walk softly or tread? Is she walking on carpet or bare floor? What kind of shoes is she wearing? Do they squeak or clack or hiss as her feet cross the floor? Does dust rise from an old carpet and tickle your nose?

Go for the details — and don't worry about how elegantly you put them down; your critic gets to fix all that later. Just *detail it up,* for as the architect Ludwig Mies van der Rohe said, "God is in the detail." Details bring your story to life. By closely observing and then recording the sights, sounds, smells, tastes, and sensations, you'll capture the details that make *an image worth* much *more than a thousand words.*

Our movies don't just grow out of our five senses, though. There's another one I call our *seventh sense*—empathy. Our empathic ability goes far beyond compassion. *Webster's Third* defines empathy as "the capacity for participating in or a vicarious experiencing of another's feelings, volitions, or ideas and sometimes another's movements to the point of executing bodily movements resembling his."

With each of our characters we have to do more than walk a mile in their moccasins. We have to enter their bodies and walk in their skin, smelling and tasting and touching and seeing and hearing the world as they do — from the inside out.

SEVENTH SENSE

Right now, I want you to stand up and get inside the body of that old man who walked into the library. I want you to *be* that old man. When you're inside his body, I want you to hold his cane and walk across your room. You are the old man.

How did you hold the cane?

If you were inside the body of a young man, would you hold the cane the same way?

What happens when we get older? Muscles lose their flexibility; the muscles above the knee get tighter. Think about the old people you know. How do they walk? Why do they shuffle? They shuffle because they're being pulled into a knee-bending position.

This requires a different grip on the cane. What happens if you're shuffling and you're holding the cane like a seventeen-year-old would? You're like Mister Magoo, tipping over. Now if you write a description of an old man walking into the room holding the cane as a young man would, what have you done? You haven't been in his body. Until you are inside a character's body, you do not know what it's like to open his door, to eat with his fork. And once you are inside that body, you automatically will describe correctly the actions of the person. They will be right.

In every story you write, you'll need to experience the world from inside the body of every single one of your characters to get the story right. Or as Eudora Welty said it in *One Writer's Beginnings*:

> Characters take on life sometimes by luck, but I suspect it is when you can write most entirely out of yourself, inside the skin, heart, mind, and soul of a person who is not yourself that a character becomes in his own right another human being on the page.

And when you do this in your clay digging, you'll notice a very intriguing thing: the world takes on a totally different aspect. You'll notice different sounds than you noticed before and things smell in ways you've never smelt before. It's very odd, really; but it is as though you've actually inserted yourself into the glove of somebody else's body.

So back to your Sarah. Put yourself into her body and walk across the room. How do "your" feet feel? Where's the weight in your body as you, Sarah, walk?

Now, how are you going to convey what you experienced in your mind's eye so that a reader can experience it, too? The only way is to *detail it up*. *Using her walker, Sarah crossed the room with great effort* doesn't evoke the dream like *One lace straggled from Sarah's tennie, whispering across the wood as she leaned into her walker and dragged her dead foot forward*. Details! Remember the details.

When it comes to hearing, tasting, touching, smelling, seeing and empathic feeling in our mind's eye, each of us is different. What's greater for you: your ability to hear the sound of the cane or to smell the old man? Do you hear his voice better than you feel the admixture of sunlight and room-dim on your skin? And how about seeing him clearly?

Try this — but only if you're not allergic to strawberries or chocolate. Imagine that you take a strawberry and you dip it into some chocolate that's just been melted in a fondue pot. Can you smell the smell of warm chocolate? Can you feel the heat around your hand as you go toward that fondue pot? Can you feel how it envelops your hand? How it comes up from the surface of the chocolate? How much heat do you feel on the top of your hand opposed to the underside? Where on your hand do you feel it most? Is there any moisture coming up over the rest of your hand? And can you feel what it feels like to dip that strawberry? Can you feel the surface tension of the chocolate as you dip it in, the suction from the chocolate as you're pulling it out? Can you see the way the chocolate coats the tip of the strawberry? Can you see the way the seeds poke through where the chocolate has dripped down? How red is that strawberry to you? Now raise it to your mouth and bite into it. Can you hear the sound of your teeth breaking the skin? Can you feel the mix of heat and cold against your teeth as they bite through? Can you taste the commingled flavors of chocolate and strawberry? What about the smell as you chew?

Some of us can smell the difference between chocolate mocha and rocky road ice cream in our mind's eye; others can't smell at all. Some of us can feel the brush of a butterfly's wing against our cheek; others couldn't feel hot sand underfoot to save their skin. And some see in minute detail in their mind's eye; others can never see a thing.

I know a person who does not see, smell, taste, touch, hear in his mind's eye. He can't image at all. Try to understand what your inner world would be like if you couldn't, say, hear a symphony or see birds flushed from a thicket in the purple-blue light of a winter morning in your mind's eye. He has a concept of the taste of strawberries, but he can't evoke it as something that's happening *as* he thinks of it. People who create images seem odd to him. He, like everyone else, expects people to be the same; we expect that we're all referencing the world in the same mode.

This difference can be disconcerting when we discover it close to home — as I did a few years back. When my son was in high school, he cooked one meal a week. One night he served me something that looked like a burrito. I tried to separate the tastes as I chewed my first bite. He misread the look on my face. "It's not very good," he said.

"No, it's fine," I said, meaning it. "I was just trying to figure out what you'd put in it."

Being my son, he said, "Guess."

I tried, but the tastes eluded me. He finally told me the ingredients — leftover mashed potatoes, crushed corn chips . . .

"That's clever," I said. I've always admired ingenuity. Even as a kid I used to create meals from scratch. My mother would say, "With you, I know the meal's either going to be good or a disaster." Over the years I got better at making it not be a disaster.

"I don't understand how you do it, Mom," he continued. "How do you, you know, just go into the kitchen and throw all those things together and come up with something that tastes good?"

"Well, I taste it in my mind's eye as I go," I said.

He looked at me as though I were weirder than he already knew me to be.

"No, really," I said. "First you get the taste of the mashed potatoes in your head. Then you add the crunched-up corn chips, mix them together, and see how they'd taste."

He continued to look at me like I'd just arrived from another planet, but that's probably exactly how I was looking at him. "You don't do that?" I said with more than a little incredulity. This, after all, was my biological offspring.

"I don't even know what you're talking about," he said.

It was one of those moments of epiphany of which James Joyce was so fond. I saw my son in a new light — not entirely glowing. But then he redeemed himself. Indicating the green-streaked sunset outside our dining-room window, he said, "But *that* I can taste. That tastes like lime sherbet."

I've got a theory that we can make a virtue out of any inadequacy. When I was in high school I discovered that I, unlike my friends, thought in pictures. Not only that, but I had to translate everything coming in as words into "my language" to remember it and everything going out into words so others could understand it. Over the years, though, I came to see that I could *trust the process:* If I just started talking and let the words flow up from the nether reaches of my brain, they'd actually make sense. I'm still rather stunned by this ability— after twenty-five years of trusting the process.

I'm sure this thinking in pictures has given me my zany sense of humor. People who think in words say the strangest things. I heard this on TV news the other night: "a big heroine bust." But then it's reciprocal. "Take it off!" I said excitedly to my friend who was looking for the right freeway exit. Not being clairvoyant, he didn't see the image of the ramp in my mind's eye. "What? You want me to strip right here?" he asked as he zipped right by the exit.

What's your inadequacy? Celebrate it because it's what will make your writing unique; it's because each of us is weak in disparate ways that our stories evoke different worlds. Think of a person who can't hear in his mind's eye, a person who's deaf in this inner space. What would the sound of the cane be like for him? He might *feel* it as a vibration under his feet as he sat in a chair, and if he wrote it that way — "the floor sent a tatoo against my foot" — someone would read it and get a body shiver just because it's a new way of saying the same old thing. His "limitation" in and of itself would give his writing that out-of-kilter feel of original writing.

It is possible, however, to develop some of our weaker inner senses, and for a writer it's worth the work.

One of the more delightful introductions I've ever had came from Dick Fleming when he presented me as the keynote speaker at the National Amateur Printers Association's 1993 conference. He said he'd first met me when he'd taken my creative writing class a couple years before. "As a teacher," he said, "she is unusual to say the least. As an example, at one of the first class sessions we had, she was talking to us not about writing, not about words, but about feeling. And she was telling us how as a writer, we had to have sensitivity. In order to give us some grasp of the idea of sensitivity, she said, `Go home and lick the wall.' I thought this was rather peculiar, but I thought, the kid's the teacher and I'm the pupil, I'll go home and try it. So I went home, and I licked the kitchen wall. It tasted like ham and eggs. Went into the living room, and there was the delicate taste of television. I went and licked the bathroom wall, and aughhhh! Anyway, it was good advice."

I confess. I do want you to lick walls, as well as various other "unwriterly" things. But there's a method to my madness. It's one of the best ways I know for you to add to your sensory repertoire — that writer's arsenal that will serve you well in the future.

I also want you to get in the habit of doing what I call a *nightly recap*. It's something I started doing as a small child. Each night as I lay in bed with the lights out, I'd remember as many details from the day as I could — basically replaying the day from morning until night in my mind. I got better and better at it. By junior high, I could remember not only the words someone said, but the way in which he or she said them — the angle of body, the tightness of face, the rhythms of sound.

It wasn't until I was in college, though, that I realized the power of this nightly recap. Because I was determined to go beyond reading French to the seemingly impossible art of speaking French, I started doing my nightly recap in French. Before long, I was dreaming in French! It was my first encounter with the power of the unconscious. It was, also, my first inkling that my nightly recap was more than a game: it was night school.

NIGHTLY RECAP

So this is what you do: lie in bed with the lights out and recall as vividly as you can as many details as you can. No paper, no pencil — you're just doing this in your head in the dark. Think through what you saw, smelled, tasted, touched, heard, and felt during the day. What exactly did the sound of that person's voice feel like to you when you came into the room and he was screaming? Don't just remember that it happened, but try to remember its affect. What part of your body tightened? How did you respond? What were other people in the room doing when this was going on? Were they tucking into themselves? Or were they sticking their chins out with their fists up? What were the postures?

And what was the room like? Who was sitting in what chair? What color was the table? What was the effect of that light on the faces of people? Where did the shadows fall on their faces? What could you feel from behind you? Cold? Heat?

Flesh out all the details. Don't just say to yourself that the wool sweater worn by the person sitting next to you smelled pungent—stretch. Where in your nose did you smell it? Did it jab on both sides behind the tip of your nose? Details! Get all of those details into your mind. This helps develop your writer's repertoire, and later you'll be able to draw from it.

In the beginning, your nightly recaps will be strongest around your inner sensing strengths. I can still recall some of my nightly recaps from preschool days. I remember the feel of the light playing on the dog's golden face, the feel of the Cheerios and of the string as I made a necklace, the feel of bacon's smell in my nose. Everything was feeling in those days, and that is still my strongest sense: just looking at stucco makes my nerves feel as though I've actually touched it. This sort of crossing of the senses is called *synaesthesia*. *The Oxford Companion to the Mind* defines synaesthesia as

> confusion between the senses: for example, some musicians experience colours for particular notes. The effect can become dramatic in some drug states, presumably through loss of normal inhibitory mechanisms which isolate the central processing of the senses.

For writers, synaesthesia is worth cultivating. Part of the joy of reading comes from experiencing things in new ways. Think about how you feel when you read something described in a way you've never felt it, seen it, tasted it before — a sunset tasting like sherbet or from that master of synaesthesia, Lawrence Durrell: "a sky of hot nude pearl" or "empty cadences of sea-water licking its own wounds" or "a single dark whiff of sound from a siren" or "leaving the gaunt rooms echoing with their perfume."

A friend once told me Oscar Wilde said that every cliché was brilliant but the wording was wrong. I've never been able to track the quotation down, but it sounds like something Wilde might have said, so I'll give him credit. As writers, we've got to *uncliché* — get the image right. Few did it better than Nathanael West. Here are a couple of his that always stir me: "the gray sky looked as if it had been rubbed with a soiled eraser" and "he buried his triangular face like the blade of a hatchet in her neck."

I think a well-chosen image is so important that I'll spend hours trying to bring the right one up out of the well. When I was writing my book *Perchance to Dream*, I was trying to describe the sensation of eating green chile. A cliché was easy: it burned the mouth or made the eater feel as though smoke were pouring from her ears or it was hot. But an uncliché took work. After many trials, this finally popped into my head: *They sat quiet for a time, chewing on the burritos, letting the green chile trot down their nerve endings and ping in their brains like pinball machines on tilt.* That's what eating green chile feels like to me, and if I'm successful at this evocative art, the image of a pinball machine on tilt will make the experience of green chile "known" to someone who's never literally experienced it.

But don't worry about unclichéing as you write. That's something to come back to in the revision process. Just get the words down; later when it's your critic's turn, it will be delighted to uncliché for you. My critic would love to get its hands on "corrugated" in the above description of the old man's face. "Cliché!" it pronounces and shoves William Least Heat Moon's "a face so gullied even the soil conservation commission couldn't have reclaimed it" into my mind to challenge me. I see my critic's point.

To uncliché we must expand our sensual bag of tricks. Do lick walls; do get down on your hands and knees and rub your forehead on the ground. Go to restaurants to eavesdrop. It's one of the best ways to start to hear voices in your mind. The key element here is play! Start approaching the world as a child. Get sensual.

Round Robin

Here's a good exercise for entering the world of the child: I call it a Round Robin after that game many of us used to play as children. It's a two-person writing exercise — a good *writing in restau-*

rants technique. Meet someone in a coffee shop or mall eating area — someplace where you'll feel free to laugh.

The assignment is to get inside the body of a four-year-old child and record the experience as registered through his or her sensory apparatus. Because the exercise works best if women stretch and enter the bodies of four-year-old boys and men, four-year-old girls, it's most effective when women pair up with women and men pair up with men.

The technique: Each of you writes a sentence on your own sheet of paper—two pieces of paper; two first sentences. It doesn't matter if it's first person (*I love spiders*) or third person (*When no one was looking, Kim hid the mixed vegetables under the rim of the plate*), and it doesn't matter how it starts. Some of the best Round Robins have started with one word: "Mom!" Once you each have written your first sentence, exchange your papers and write your second sentence under your partner's first sentence. Now exchange again so that each of you writes your third line on the sheet of paper you had originally. Continue exchanging and writing sentences for at least ten minutes.

The goal of the Round Robin is to get as many taste, touch, smell, sight, and hearing images into your writing as you can. If your little boy hates worms, describe the sensation of hate: *his eyes burned so hot he could have torched them just by looking at them.* Really get into the experience of the experience! This is a very sensory age — things taste and things feel and things goo and things yuck. If you're really in the child's body, this will come out as you chronicle.

People have asked me why the Round Robin is a two-person exercise. The reason is this: If it were a one-person exercise, you'd have a chance to think. Instead you'll read what your partner has written and say to yourself, "Why did she write that line? It isn't what I had in mind." And because it isn't what you "had in mind," you'll find yourself chronicling the movies in the mind instead. When you can't *think to it,* you'll be able to get an idea of what happens when you do move out of your own way and trust the process.

Another thing people have asked me is why women should write from inside the boy and men from inside the girl? It's because it's easier to write evocatively from the experience of another. Writing from our own experience becomes a sort of shorthand: we leave out half of it because it's so well known. But when you're writing from inside a not-self character, you don't leave out that crucial information because you don't know it until you experience it. It's brand new. It's not just remembering what the world was like when you were a little kid. It's experiencing the world fresh through the eyes and ears and fingers and skin and nose and mouth of a small child and chronicling the movies in our mind so that a reader can experience it, too.

That's art.

INCREASING YOUR SENSORY REPERTOIRE

Don't stop with licking walls or rubbing your forehead against the carpet. Notice what it feels like. Get creative: encounter the world as you might have as a kid. Then find someone to do Round Robins with. And remember to do a Nightly Recap every single night. It's the best writer's tool there is.

CHAPTER THREE

PARTICIPATORY ART

In *Poetics*, Aristotle wrote: *"the pleasure the poet is to provide is that which comes from pity and fear."* As long as it's not our own problems we're emoting over, feeling pity and fear does give pleasure — so much so that it's the source of the two essentials in all fiction: the need to engage your reader in your character's plight and the need for suspense.

Ancient Greek playwrights worked hard to evoke strong emotions in the bodies of those watching their plays. If you think about Greek drama, it's rather interesting that they could do so. The audience knew the storyline before the play started: Greek drama used the old tales over and over again. And the actors were hardly what we'd call actors today: they wore masks and declaimed their lines. How could the play move the audience to emotions so intense as pity and fear? Simple: The ancient Greeks knew the power of rhythm to evoke emotion.

Think about some of the movies that have affected you the most. If you could watch them without the music track, would their impact be as profound? I doubt it. At least half of a good movie's power comes from the music. What would *Chariots of Fire* have been without Vangelis' score? How much credit does John Barry deserve for the impact of *Dances with Wolves*? Like the Greek dramatists, the best film producers know the body is the instrument on which music plays. A chord is bowed and we know a thrill of fear; another, and sentiment for the stuckness of the human condition weights us into remembrance.

Maybe that's why we say it "sings" when we get the story right. The emotions feel apt. And when the story's "good but not quite there," we get things like Leo Cullum's cartoon in the January 18, 1993 *The New Yorker* where an editor with a huge manuscript tells the writer that he should now "make it sing."

Making it sing isn't such a hard task as it seems if you're accurately writing from the inside out. Consider this for a moment. I'm angry, but I don't want you to know I'm angry, and you ask me, "Are you mad?" I'd put a smile on my face and say, "Mad? I'm Not Mad! What Makes You Think I'm Mad?" And you'd think, "Unhunh, she's mad." How would you know that? Right: my sentences are choppy. When we're mad, we talk choppy. We can't hide it: our rhythm gives us away because rhythm *is* emotion.

Emotion, though, is a two-sided coin. It is absolutely impossible to have an emotion in your body without having a concomitant sensory image in your mind's eye — and vice versa. In my workshops, I use a couple of anecdotes to illustrate. Here's a transcript of one:

> Close your eyes. I'm going to tell you a story. I want you to imagine that you're in a little chapel. The doors are open and it's really sunny. It's a nice, beautiful day, and people are coming in dressed in beautiful summer clothes, hats and all. Along the walls there are big bouquets of flowers. People are filling the pews, and it doesn't take you long to figure out that you're at a wedding. So squeeze over into the corner of a pew and try to make yourself invisible. The minister comes in, and the groom comes to stand next to him, and the best man stands with him, and then you hear the wedding march from the loft above. In through that open doorway comes the bride. Now her dress is so wide that her father has to walk slightly behind her, and as she walks along the pews, her dress brushes. She gets up to the front, climbs the one little step, stands next to her husband-to-be. The ceremony starts. When they get to the part where the bride is asked if she takes this man to be her lawfully wedded husband, she turns to the congregation assembled and she says, "No. There is no way I would marry this man. Last night I found him in bed with my maid of honor, and I am not marrying this man." And she walks down the aisle and straight out the door.

By this point in this very bald story, people are laughing. I ask the group, "What happened inside your body when she said no?"

Some describe it as an effervescence in their belly; others as an "uummph of release."

This is the way a joke works. It affects you viscerally and that visceral sensation leads to laughter. You're listening; you're imaging along; and because you're imaging along, you're feeling in your body. Then the punch line opens the door to something completely unexpected. It's that reversal of your expectation that causes sensations in your body, which creates that release that's a laugh.

Here's the second anecdote:

> Close your eyes. You are sitting outside a hot dog stand on a busy city street. A hot dog stand. Outside. Eating. And all of a sudden you hear the sound of cars colliding, and in that instant, just as you're turning, you hear a woman shriek, "My baby!"

What happens inside of you when you hear those words in your mind's eye? Try imaging it again, more vividly. Watch the way the feeling plays through you. Does your stomach knot? Do chills course over your body? It's not the words that make you feel; it's the fact that you're imaging — hearing the words in your mind's eye. If you merely read the words without imaging the scene, you wouldn't feel anything.

For instance, read this word without imaging: Popsicle.

Now lick a Popsicle in your mind's eye.

Read: Oatmeal cookies.

Now smell the smell of oatmeal cookies baking.

Read: Bread.

Now watch butter melt on a hot piece of bread fresh from the oven.

Read: Ferris wheel.

Now feel the Ferris wheel rock as it climbs its circle through the night sky.

An image is worth much more than a thousand words because it produces:

> a physiological departure from homeostasis that is subjectively experienced in strong feelings (as of love, hate, desire,

or fear) and manifests itself in neuromuscular, respiratory, cardiovascular, hormonal, and other bodily changes preparatory to overt acts which may or may not be performed" (emotion as defined by *Webster's Third*)

Fiction's power comes from the fact that when our readers are feeling and tasting and touching and seeing and hearing in their mind's eye, they're experiencing emotions in their bodies.

The simple biological reason for this is the limbic system. "Encircling the brainstem with a `wishbone' structure," say the authors of *The Brain: A User's Manual*, "the limbic system is a mini brain handling emotions and involved in memory." Limbic means "bordering," which is what it does — sits on top of the brainstem below the evolved new brain. It is the oldest part of the new brain. "Indeed man's limbic system shows little difference from that of primitive mammals — hence its nickname: `old mammalian brain.'"

Emotions and memory. And what's memory? When it comes to the oldest part of the new brain, we're not talking about words or concepts or mathematical ideas. No, we're talking about images.

Other mammals don't have our evolved cerebral cortex, but they do share with us this "old mammalian brain" that feels emotions and that dreams. This is the storymaker part of the brain, the part of the brain we're dealing with in this *movies in the mind* process.

The question, though, is how do we as writers capitalize on this image/emotion coin to make our readers feel? I came across the answer when I was a University of Chicago creative writing student in search of a subject for my master's dissertation. Like many students of writing, I'd become highly sensitized to language, so much so that movies had largely become words for me. I remember seeing one that had such "nothing" words that I was surprised by their emotional punch. It made no sense. But then I thought that maybe what was happening was that by some osmotic process the writer had captured his emotion in these seemingly non-emotional words. And that was the seed idea for my dissertation.

I took my second step toward it when I rounded a corner at the Hirshhorn Museum in Washington, D.C. There, in a spot of sunlight on a clean curve of wall, hung a wail of grief. At least, that's how my body responded in the instant I saw the bronze sculpture on the wall: I felt a wrench of pain inside my breast — the wrench that comes, I know now, with a mourning wail. And yet it was only a small bronze relief of a woman's face — maybe fifteen by fifteen inches. How had that small piece of metal produced such an instantaneous and powerful reaction in me?

The woman's eyes were closed, so it was not from them that the sense of insurmountable pain was communicated. And scarcely any of the woman's face showed: The left hand covered the left eye and cheek, and the right covered the mouth and left hand. The thumb from the right hand stretched along the right side of the face to the ear. Certainly the hands told a story, but was it enough to produce such a reaction in me? No, it was obviously a case of the whole being greater than the sum of the parts. The only thing I understood was that the artist had known this choked scream of pain.

Before I moved on, I looked at the nameplate. The bronze was called "Grief" or "Lament" in English. And the artist was Käthe Kollwitz. Most who know the Prussia-born Kollwitz's work at all know it from her famous "Never Again War" poster — a shout aimed at Hitler as he pulled Germany toward yet another war. Her anti-war sentiment caused her dismissal from the Prussian Academy of Arts in Berlin, where she had been the director of the master classes in graphic arts. Interestingly, her art wasn't destroyed, but consigned to the academy's basement. She lived through the war, dying of natural causes in April 1945.

But she had experienced the pain. In 1914, her son Peter had died on a Flanders' field. In fact, it took ten years after his death for Kollwitz to return to her art, and she wrote later that it was her art that kept her alive — a line said by my Kollwitz-inspired character in my novel *Perchance to Dream*. Yes, this record of her pain and the pain of those around her kept her alive. It also transferred that pain as if by osmosis in that moment I rounded the corner in the Hirshhorn. Even though I had not lost a child or anyone close enough to me to know that wail of grief, I could feel the emotion as strongly as though it were my own. How was that possible? How could I experience an emotion I'd never known?

Art that evokes a feeling in the viewer, the audience, or the reader that is similar to the feeling the artist had when creating the work I named *participatory art*. The two experiences — the movie and Kollwitz's sculpture — set a wheel in motion: my subject for my dissertation would be participatory art.

I knew from my work in drama that a concept similar to participatory art had been around for a long time. At the turn of the century, the great Russian director Constantin Stanislavski revolutionized drama by moving it away from the oratorical style so popular at that time to what we think of as acting today: an actor playing the part of a character so convincingly that we believe the actor and the character to be one.

Before Stanislavski's revolution, theater had been declaimed as in Shakespeare's day when his four-hour-long plays were said at a romp, actors moving little and using their hands in stylized gestures to help convey the play's meaning to an often rowdy and under-educated audience. Little had changed: in Stanislavski's time, great oratory was still the thing.

"No!" bellowed Stanislavski in response to this. On his famous Moscow Arts Theatre stage, he brought Anton Chekhov's plays to the world not as oratory but as real life. His technique, which we call *method acting* today, amounted to this: If, for instance, an actor had to play the part of a person whose father was dying there on the stage, she was to hold in her mind's eye the memory of her own father's death. And if her father hadn't died, she was to hold in her mind's eye the death of another person whose passing would be as powerfully felt. And if no one close to her had died, she was to remember vividly carrying the limp body of her dog that had just been run over by a carriage wheel. Then with one of these memories vivid in her mind's eye, she was to walk across the stage and say as she sunk to her father's death bed, "Don't die." The emotion remembered, claimed Stanislavski, would color the way she walked, the way she held her body, the way she said her lines. Thus the audience would believe that what they were watching was real: the rhythm played out in her step and her words would convince them of the veracity. They would believe because emotion made it true.

Sometimes this is easier said than done. When I played Laura in *The Glass Menagerie,* I had a hard time bringing her to life. Laura is a wilting flower of a shy person, which I had never been in my life. It was a real stretch to find an image that imprinted my body with shyness. Finally it rose from the well: the vision of a portrait by Whistler of a young woman dressed in white. It hangs in the National Gallery in Washington, D.C., but at that time, I had only seen it in an art book of my mother's that I'd studied endlessly as a child. When I tracked the picture down, I knew it was just what I needed to bring Laura to life in my body because for me it was a hauntingly beautiful evocation of everything it is to be shy. And at times on the stage it worked too well: I found myself whispering!

Method acting uses the image/emotion coin to create rhythm in the actors' words and actions and thus make the parts they're playing believable. I wanted to take it one step further: I wanted to prove that beyond producing an affect in the artist, it was possible to produce the *same* emotion in the viewer, reader, or audience in much the same way Kollwitz's sculpture had produced grief in me.

To that end, I designed a participatory art experiment where I would write from a strong emotion, chronicling what I experienced in my mind's eye, and I would write only if I felt that emotion strongly as a bodily sensation *while* I was writing. If I stopped feeling at any time and flipped into the tip-of-the-iceberg-type writing, I would quit writing and wait until I got the feeling in my body back. I called this *method writing* to honor its source. If I did my method writing successfully, I reasoned, I could produce in my dissertation advisor the same emotion I felt when I wrote: he would be a participant in the experience, rather than a bystander.

Although I could have done method writing from any emotion, because I was experiencing a difficult period in my life, I decided to choose an emotion I wanted to spend time with: I picked joy. What I mean by joy isn't the "oh, gee, isn't that fun" feeling, but that awe-filled, transformative feeling that comes usually from the little moments in life — a sudden glimpse of sun streaking down through clouds, the sound of a baby's laughter, the smell of a first snow. Or like the time when I was taking a bath and raised my head up from under the water, opening my eyes to see rainbows dancing in the droplets caught on my lashes. In that moment, I felt a sun rising in my chest and melted silver running cool through my body

— that's how joy feels to me. But everyone is different, so you have to discover what your joy sensation is like so you can "name" it and get back to it easily.

Every day during my experiment of method writing, I would sit and remember a time like this. As soon as an image like that of the rainbow balls dancing in my lashes came into my mind's eye, the feeling of joy would again fill my body. It's then that I'd write, describing what I saw, felt, touched, tasted, heard. If the feeling went away, I'd stop writing and wait for it to come back. Then I'd write again.

It wasn't long before I ran out of joy memories. What to do? That's when I discovered that it went both ways: if I merely recalled how joy felt in my body, the sensation remembered viscerally would produce an image in my mind's eye. And sometimes it would surprise me what came up from the well — like this memory of sitting on the edge of a church hall during a small New Mexico town's *fiesta*:

> The dancers danced the floor dust swirling up from it to my nostrils as I sat cross-legged on the edge of it and watched as the dancers danced to my knees feet stomping rhythms that made my body bounce. There on the floor as the dancers danced to my knees, knives clacking unbroken beats on the wooden floor beneath me. There I watched as the dancers danced, the dust swirled, the knives clacking as feet bounced above them, around them as the dancers danced at my knees I watched, body bouncing around me.

Even reading now, the feeling of joy returns. And my critic is nudging me to revise — "take out the its; add commas." But my project didn't allow revision because to revise would have potentially destroyed the rhythm I hoped the emotion had imprinted on the page.

At the end of my experiment, I collected the best of these *joy writings*, titled them *Painted Images*, and turned them in to my dissertation advisor, who was expecting only a collection of prose poems. I figured if he knew what I was up to, he'd make a very poor test subject.

On his critique he wrote, "I enjoyed reading these."

Enjoyed. Yes! I thought. Participatory art!

Even though there was nothing in these prose poems for him to know he should feel *joy*, he did. Like Kollwitz's sculpture, the effect was greater than the sum of the individual parts.

JOY WRITING

Right now, I'd like you to stop reading and do a joy writing.

What does joy feel like? When I ask people that question they usually raise their arms up from the sides as if embracing the sun. Make that physical motion. Do it a couple of times. What happens in your body when you do that? Is there a sense of diaphragm involvement, opening up, expansion? That feeling is what I'm talking about: joy. When you made that movement were there any memories triggered? When I did it just now, I was a little kid on a swing. I loved that feeling as a kid.

Next I want you to spend fifteen minutes doing joy writing. You can actually write from any emotion you want to, but writing from the feeling of joy is fun. You can start with either image or emotion, because as you've seen they are two sides of the same coin:image/emotion. You can start with remembering a time in your life when you know you were joyful — the day you got married if that was a joyful day; some time when you were a little kid helping to make the oatmeal cookies if that triggered a joy reaction in you. Anything. Or if you can't think of a time off the top of your head, remember the feeling. And if you remember the feeling vividly, an image is going to come into your mind's eye. Remember these are not the Big Events of life but those moments where things are almost like a cosmic joke: all of a sudden everything's so brilliant.

For the next fifteen minutes, as you immerse yourself in feeling joy, and you're vividly remembering, then write as you feel in your body. Don't write otherwise. If that feeling goes away, get the images back, get the body sensation back, and then write. It doesn't matter if you only write one line. It matters that that line comes out of the body sensation, that you're actually there as you write.

Some of the writing that comes out of these exercises is awe-inspiring. This was written by Dr. Avrum Organick during a workshop in Albuquerque:

> I was thirteen. The sun was at its height at the summer solstice. I had dreamed about riding a bicycle, how I would lean into a curve going around a corner, how I would feel the breeze in my face, how I would have the certainty that I would not fall. Yet I had never ridden a bicycle until that moment. It was a girl's bicycle, my cousin Edith's, so I had the assurance I could get off of it easily if I started to fall. But I didn't fall. I kept right on going. I felt the breeze in my face just as in the dream. I felt the confidence I had in my own dream. I felt the power in my legs as I pumped forward. Suddenly the world opened up all around me. The sun shone down on the tall hedges along the road. God was there! I knew it; I felt it in the joy I had with every breath. I had never known such joy before. I had never felt the presence of God before. I have had joy since, many times, and I was happy to have had joy again, but never again was there that powerful presence of God. I am happy with the idea of God, but I have never felt him again as I had that day on Edith's bicycle

Avrum went on to turn this joy writing into an exceptionally profound essay.

Sometimes joy writing goes beyond awe-inspiring to downright useful. In one workshop, I watched a woman get more and more excited as she wrote; her face told a story! After the fifteen minutes were up, I said, "Would you like to read what you wrote?"

"No," she said. "It's a bit too personal. But I will tell you this: it'll make a great anniversary present for my husband."

That reminded me of a time I was fully immersed in writing a sex scene. There was a tap on my door, and my husband stuck his head around the corner. "Are you busy?" he asked in his most seductive voice.

The power of participatory art!

When we're writing from the inside out like this, not only is the rhythm of the words affected by the image/emotion coin, but also the words we choose. We don't have to select our verbs and adjectives consciously; if we're experiencing emotion in our body, the words will be right. And conversely if we've entered the body of our character, then the character's emotions will cause us to use the right words. For instance, imagine you are in the body of Francisco Pizarro, the conqueror of Peru, who took all the Incan sites but for Machu Picchu. Imagine you're in Pizarro's body and you're riding on his great horse into Cuzco, having just captured this village. Can you feel that horse under you? The heat of the sun? The thinness of the Andean air? You ride straight to the plaza and dismount. Can you feel yourself getting off that horse, Pizarro? You get off the horse and you hand the reins to the boy standing there and then you skip across the plaza.

No? Obviously, you'd have had to leave his body to skip across the plaza. How does the body of Pizarro, the conqueror of Peru, move across the plaza? Feel the center of gravity in his chest? Feel the arrogance? Is his walk a skip? No, more like a stride. Get it down. Write down the word "stride," and then later, if you think that's too much a cliché, let your critic turn it into its most beautiful form. That's the critic's job — to climb back into Pizarro's body and shape the writing until it sings! Your storymaker at least got the essence right!

The image/emotion coin leaves its trail in the details as well. If you're in Pizarro's body feeling that arrogance as he strides across the plaza, would you see a flower? Only if it were clutched to the breast of a terrified woman — and you'd see it like a slash of blood.

Method writing is to write from anger. It is to write from happiness. It is to write from that bittersweet feeling that we're unfamiliar with in this culture. The 1968 Nobel Prize for Literature winner Yasunari Kawabata wrote a book that evokes this bittersweet feeling. It's called *Beauty and Sadness* in translation, but I believe the Japanese might have one pictograph for what we need two words to describe: the sense that with beauty comes exquisite sadness and with sadness comes exquisite beauty. Write from that inescapable fusion the word "bittersweet" points to. Write from any emotion — rage, playfulness, longing, anticipation, angst — and write from memories when those memories trigger emotions in your body.

Method writing will take you directly to the source: you'll be surprised by what will come up from the well when you're immersed in the feeling, chronicling the movies in the mind. Often what comes are the details recorded if you have kept a journal — details you think you want to remember because you might use them in a story some day. I've come to the conclusion that though a journal is an important writer's tool, it's not the only repository of story material; that material is all there — stored in the unconscious — and when we need it, it springs up to fit itself to the story. Writing from the inside out is often an experience of saying "Wow! I'd forgotten all about that" when some jewel inserts itself at just the right place on the line. It's half of what makes writing fun: nothing's ever lost.

I wrote my novel *Perchance to Dream* with method writing. The excerps below came from recalling moments on my grandparents' farm. It was a place of great joy for me, and if there's a heaven . . .

Perchance to Dream is a magical realism story of a seventy-two-year-old artist Bergen Klein who's dead but doesn't know that she's dead. The experiences in the book happen on that temporary afterlife plane the Tibetan Buddhists call the Bardo, and the story's full of ideas of parallel universes and reincarnation. In chapter eleven, Bergen encounters her doppelgänger, and in this double's eyes she sees moments from her (their?) childhood.

In her double's eyes, Bergen saw the road to her grandma and grandpa's house. The seat she sat on swayed with the motion of the wheels over the deep-rutted ground. "EeeYup!" said the driver, clicking his tongue as he slapped the reins lightly on the backs of two white horses whose shoulders were almost as high as the swaying seat.

"Me," said the little girl sitting next to the driver, her hair swinging back and forth against the sides of her face. "Me. Let me do that."

"No, Miss Bergen. That's nothing for a tiny girl to be doing. Them horses if they get away, why they'll tip this wagon for sure. They's big ones, *ja*?"

"Just for a bit?"

"No, it won't do you no good to use your city ways on me, miss. When a man says no, it's no he means for sure," said the driver as he flipped the reins leaning forward toward the horses. "Look past them trees. See there, your grandpa's house?"

The house stood shining silver in the sun.

"It's very pretty," said Bergen.

"Pretty!" snorted the driver. "Logs, they're not pretty. That is just the sun's trick to make you think you are coming home to heaven."

Bergen watched the house grow bigger as the horses rocked the wagon down the hill. "Whoaaa!" shouted the driver, pulling back on the reins. "Whoaaa, Belle. Hold up there, Star."

"Dowwwnnnnnnn!" sang the child as the wagon bumped fast after the cantering horses.

"They can smell them oats," said the man. "Whoaaa! Hungry beggars aren't you? Whoaaa!"

"Dowwwnnnnnnn!" called Bergen as they rolled toward her grandparents' house. "Dowwwnnnnnnnnnn!"

"Whoaaa, now, whoaaa. We got to turn this corner at a decent speed," said the man, but the horses raced into the long drive toward the house, tipping the wagon onto the two wheels on Bergen's side, nearly dumping her into the ditch. "Hold on, child. Whoaa!"

Bergen grabbed tight to the back of the seat and to the metal handhold at her side. Her teeth chattered with each fast bump of the wagon, and her eyes bounced fuzzy over the figure running out of the house, toward the wagon.

"Your grandpa," shouted the man to Bergen as he pulled tight on the reins. Olaf ran toward them, his arms upraised and waving. The horses shied, slowed, and trotted, snorting, toward the house.

"Got some runaways there," said Olaf as he swung into the wagon and chucked Bergen under the chin. "You come home to grandpa, Bergie?" His laughing blue eyes caught hers and tugged like a buttonhook at the tip of her spine. She giggled.

"What's my girl laughing about?" he asked as he hugged her to him as the wagon rolled toward the house.

"Your eyes tickle me inside," she said. "All the way down."

Olaf threw back his head and roared with laughter. "Hother, you hear this granddaughter of mine? A splash of aquavit, *ja*?"

"She wanted to drive them horses," said Hother.

"She did, did she?" said Olaf, squeezing Bergen tight. "Just like her grandma, is she?"

"Sure see a touch," said Hother as he pulled the horses right toward the barn, and tugged back hard on the reins. "Hold up, now."

As the horses stopped, Olaf hopped to the ground and reached his arms up to Bergen. She jumped into his hands, and her white skirt belled wide with air and landed in the pupils of the *doppelgänger*'s eyes.

The second exerpt:

And in her double's eyes, Bergen saw lace curtains billowing out over the bed and brushing back to the window. Again the wind lifted them, and they floated up, the hem tickling the child's face as they drifted by. Bergen woke and rubbed her nose. Above her the curtain played, and the sun, dusting through it, scattered laced light across the ceiling and on the back of her hands as it rode the wind's breath, tickling past her, sucked back into the open window.

Downstairs the screen door slapped, and footsteps crossed to the bottom of the stairs. "Time to get up, you sleepyhead!" called Nina, her voice circling up the stairs like the lines on a barbershop pole.

"Up! Up! Up!" Bergen sang back, matching her words with the wind pushing the curtain high toward the ceiling. As the curtain fell back toward the window, Bergen bounced to her knees so the lace clung to her. She laughed and stuck her head out the window. The sun slipped soft, gentle as her mother's hands, over her head. Tears filled her eyes and dropped like snowflakes to the grass far below.

"Breakfast," called Nina from the stairwell. "Come and get it."

As Bergen dipped under the curtain, a voice filled her head.

"I love you."

"Momma?" said Bergen as she looked fast around the room.

No one was there.

"Bergen."

She looked through the shadow of lace out toward the pine trees that stood on the North side of the house.

"I love you."

There, sitting high in one of the pines, was an eagle, bright as a $20 gold piece in the morning light.

"Bergen, I love you."

"Momma?"

The eagle cocked its head from side to side.

"You look like a chicken when you do that!" said Bergen, laughing as she fell backward into the down, her white nightgown covering her head.

In writing this chapter, I allowed the memory to be so keen that I felt each thing vividly as I wrote it. This is not to say that everything happened. As a child I did wake in the room where Bergen woke and hear the noise from below and watch the curtains billow with the wind scented with alfalfa (just writing this line stirs joy in me). However, I've never seen an eagle in that pine tree. But early one morning my grandpa stopped his old car on the way to church so we could all get out and look at the eagle sitting in the arbor of trees over the road. It was a powerful memory, and I drew on it to give a veracity to the words I was writing when describing Bergen talking with the eagle in the pine tree. Fiction is like that: a combination of the real and the imagined; the as-it-was and the re-arranged. For all of it, though, whether it's coming from our memory or our imagination, the technique's the same: we must enter the movies in the mind so vividly that they imprint their emotion on our body. Then the words that come off our pen carry that rhythm and sing their song to the body of our reader. That's fiction's power; that's participatory art.

 METHOD WRITING

I want you to do method writing for at least fifteen minutes every day. One day write from anger; the next write from that bittersweet feeling. Write from grief, happiness, rage, ecstasy. Just keep chronicling the movies in the mind, but remember, only write when you feel the emotion *in your body*.

CHAPTER FOUR

DIGGING THE CLAY

Get used to the question, "Where do you get your stories?" It's one you will often be asked. The best answer I've ever heard came from Anton Chekhov by way of Francine Prose. In her article "Learning from Chekhov" she writes, "Once when someone asked him about his method of composition, Chekhov picked up an ashtray. `This is my method of composition,' he said. `Tomorrow I will write a story called "The Ashtray." ' " Pick an image, any image; for an image is a seed out of which the story grows.

Usually, the image is a remembered moment in time — a little incident that burns itself on our memory. William Faulkner began *The Sound and the Fury* from the image of a little girl with dirty pants looking into a room where her brothers played. Katherine Anne Porter's "Flowering Judas" took root in her while she was living in Mexico just after the Obregón revolution.

> The idea first came to me one evening when going to visit the girl I call Laura in the story, I passed the open window of her living room on my way to the door, through the small patio which is one of the scenes in the story. I had a brief glimpse of her sitting with an open book in her lap, but not reading, with a fixed look of pained melancholy and confusion in her face. The fat man I call Braggioni was playing the guitar and singing to her.

It took a dozen years for this image seed to come to fruition in "Flowering Judas," but, said Porter, "If I had not seen her face at that very moment, I should never have written just this story because I should not have known it to write."

It's images that haunt us, that remind themselves to us over and over again, that carry our stories.

But what if you don't have any images nudging at you? Where do you find *your* stories? Because of the image/emotion coin, method writing is a great source. Look at the method writing you did: You'll probably have at least one tale rearing its head, screaming to be told.

Ah, but what if this stuff of stories still isn't hitting you over the head? Where do you look for the story in search of an author? Images are all around us. Take a look at the articles and photographs in a newspaper. If one resonates with you, clip it; it may contain a story that's yours to tell. I clipped a photo from the October 1, 1989 *New York Times* with this cutline:

> Through the fence of the West German Embassy in Prague, a mother who planned to return to East Germany said goodbye to her daughter, who was among the more than 3,500 refugees given permission yesterday to emigrate to the West.

This photo of mother and teenage-looking daughter, foreheads and hands touching through the fence, tugged at my heart. I know what it's like to be separated from one's child by forces bigger than oneself. From this image, I could write a story.

But writers find their stories anywhere and everywhere. In Salvatore La Puma's short story "Inside the Fire," he tells of a birthday party cum wedding given by the homeless for one of their own. One of the main characters is Sergio, an out-of-work comedian. At the bottom of the third page comes what I think was the image seed for the story:

> The audience in the nightclub where he had last worked also hadn't laughed when he made up a story about a homeless guy who gave a birthday party for a bag lady, and now he himself was going to be a character in that story except that it wasn't fiction anymore.

I don't know that this is how it happened for La Puma, but I can imagine his hearing this joke and thinking, "Wouldn't that make a great story!" And in the hands of a master like La Puma, it does.

Sometimes these images cause the story to spring to life quickly, but sometimes they work in our unconscious for years until the stories seem to write themselves and pop out whole cloth — as happened with Porter "between seven o'clock and midnight of a very cold December, 1929, in Brooklyn" a dozen years after seeing "Laura's" pained face. That's what happened with my story "God's Will." An image seed kept reminding itself to me over and over like little drifts of memory coming up out of the well. I couldn't shake it. It haunted me. Finally the story had to be told.

The first version of "God's Will" grew from an image seed of a kitten. But I'm getting ahead of the story.

In the summer of 1981, I was burnt out. I'd just finished my graduate course work, and I should have been studying for my comps. Instead I took a busman's holiday at the Aspen Writers' Conference. Our group's leader, Marilyn Krysl, didn't see it as a holiday, though. She'd given us an assignment to produce a short story before the two weeks were up. Hard as I tried, a new story eluded my fried brain.

The deadline came closer. What to write when the well's run dry? Because I'd been studying and teaching the workings of the unconscious for a long time, I knew that if I found an image and went to bed and slept on it, in the morning I was probably going to have, if not a story, at least a start of a story. But what image?

Immediately Nut came into my mind — a little black shadow of a cat that thought she was my firstborn. And it wasn't surprising that this particular incident surfaced. I'd been reminded of it over and over again for a decade. I'd always wanted to use it in a story, but as you'll see, it's an anecdote, lacking the stuff of stories.

It happened like this: In 1971, my husband and I had gone to Australia on their assisted-passage program. It was Christmastime, I was four months pregnant, and we were living in the hostel in Sydney along with all the other emigrés. We nicknamed it "the hostile" — a converted army camp complete with barracks, latrines, and a mess hall. One night I left my husband in the mess, sipping his sugared milk tea with the Dutch and Chileans and Venezuelans who had become our friends, and I walked back through what was truly a dark and stormy night to our ten-by-seven-foot room.

I was feeling about as low as I get, and didn't notice at first the cat who had glommed on to my leg. It was a persistent thing, though; it literally pressed its side into my calf as we made our way through the cold rain. When I opened the door to the room, there was no question I was being asked to give a room for the night. I turned up the gas heater; the cat curled beside it, and I stretched beside both on the twin-size bed my husband and I shared.

He came back from the mess, acknowledged the cat, and settled beside me to sleep. I read. Sometimes there do seem to be these little cosmic jokes . . . That night I was reading Irving Stone's *The Agony and the Ecstasy*.

I read. Before long I realized the cat was watching me. It was unnerving. I stared back. Soon I noticed what looked to be a contraction. But that was totally implausible. Cats find dim corners to give birth in — not the center of a room. I read on. The cat watched me. Soon I realized she was in labor, and she was doing more than watching me: She was asking for help.

I got down on my knees beside her and actually pulled the kitten out of her. She licked this small black ball, and I waited for the rest. But no other kittens and no afterbirth came. Finally I went to sleep.

In the morning, there was this one little kitten. And that's how Nut became my firstborn — at least in her mind. She followed me everywhere like the ducklings Konrad Lorenz imprinted. As I got bigger in belly with my pregnancy, she'd settle on the rounding shelf under my breasts. The heat from her body would make my son kick, and she'd look around trying to find the source of the insult. She was exceedingly jealous when the one I thought was my first-born came home from the hospital. But she got her revenge: my son's seriously allergic to cats to this day.

Nut's birth was the image that came to me that night. I'd often thought to write about it, but I never saw how I could move it from vignette to story. I knew enough, though, not to argue with the creative process. I took what was offered and slept on it.

In the morning I woke to an empty house (*oh joy, oh joy!*) and started writing the moment I got up. These were the words that came out:

All his life he'd been a good man. Or so he thought. He'd farmed this land, dry, flat, nothing land. He worked hard every day, out here riding up and down these rows on his tractor — when he got one. He was a hardworking man.

He had a son and his son was given to playing. They lived far enough from people that the boy had been saved from doing it too frequently. He was a tall boy, lean, with dark hair. He had his mother's eyes. Wild eyes.

His mother died when the boy was born. She died when she was pushing him out. He was stuck with only his head out when the contractions stopped. She'd been clawing the bedpost, cursing him this child when she died. He'd had to dig in with his hands, up into that slippery, cooling space, and pull the child with all his might. There was a suction that pulled the child back. He'd pull, as gently as his man's hands could let him. Gentle, but firm pulls, but the suction would slide the child back in. The child was crying already, and that was good — he wouldn't have to worry about cleaning him out. It took a mighty thrust and pull, but finally he got the child out. He left the afterbirth in her. He had no roses to feed.

The baby boy grew. He fed him goat's milk, making a teat from an old bit of cloth as he'd done for the animals that lost their mum. He'd raised the boy, named the boy. He named the boy Will as his father had named him Justice.

They lived together, alone, in a shack that was all, said Justice, a man needed. It had the one room with beds, a table, an old wood cook stove. In the corner were boxes where they kept their clothes and dishes. The place had no windows — good to keep the dust out, said Justice — and only one door that was so low that even Justice had to stoop to get through it. The pump was outside, the privy was out back. There was no porch, no welcome mat. His wife had never been happy here, said it was no place for a woman. Justice agreed.

They had met at a party where he'd gone to get a wife. She had long black hair that she let fly down her back, and skin pale as moonlight. She was a beauty, but he'd take her. Her body was big enough for hard work.

It took him a year to get her. Her father was a stubborn fool, thought she could do better. But Justice wooed her with his maleness; his strength and his silence. She liked to imagine what he was feeling, and out of his silence, she'd created the man she'd always wanted. She'd have no other. She was pregnant before she convinced her father. Then he had to let her go.

Justice was a hard lover, taking her the way he roped a calf for branding, usually on the floor. She'd never had a man before, but she thought it could be different. She suggested it once and he'd slapped her, spitting out the one word, "Whore." That's when she'd learned to be silent. He wasn't a big man, but his roughed hands hurt.

He didn't want her in the house; he wanted her in the field where the work was. He called her hat a vanity, but he let her wear it because she was pregnant. It was his one kindness.

She'd move along the rows that he'd plowed, pulling the weeds, watching the canceled life — worms, bugs, sometimes a nest of rabbits — in each furrowed mound. If she watched too long, he'd bellow back at her, a bull ready to charge. She'd move faster down the length of the field, crawling along the earth, her full belly dragging the ground. Her son wasn't like her, he never forgot how to feel, he never let Justice knock it out of him.

The boy grew, taller than his father, bigger. By the time he was ten, he was too big for his father to hit him. Then Justice got him in other ways. He took the door off the privy where Will went to be alone.

But Justice would go into town once a month, leaving Will at home. That's when Will taught himself to drive the tractor.

Justice had never let him drive the tractor. It was his one pride, a gift his father-in-law had given them at their marriage. He'd ride the perforated metal seat with his back straight, riding the swing of the seat as the big wheels fought the rocky ground. It was a power that made him bigger than himself, and Justice rode it tall.

Justice would leave for town, and Will would practice, his feet pumping the pedals, his hands curling around the knuckle grooves on the black rubber wheel. He learned to shift the gears and aim the tires, and by the time he was twelve he was brave enough to get it going, moving across the field in the tracks Justice had cut, so his father would never know he'd had it out, was riding the cut metal seat, sitting higher than Justice ever could sit.

By the time Will was fourteen, his chest was a prize-fighter's, his neck a young bull's. He had hair dark as night-time without a moon, and his eyes were still wild unless he looked at Justice. Then they were cold.

One day, Justice was gone and Will cut new tracks, wheeling the heavy machine wherever he wanted it to go. By the time Justice got home, the field was cut in circles, the crop they'd planted, gone. The tractor with Will sitting on it, was in the middle, engine idling, nose pointed tight on

Justice who walked toward the boy he'd called his son. When Justice was a few feet from him, Will slammed the clutch and let the tractor roll. The last thing Justice saw was his tractor moving over him and the boy smiling with his wife's eyes.

There's a long distance from Nut's birth to this telling I called "Tractor." Where had this come from? But I knew. It wasn't a story unknown to me.

The events of "Tractor" came to me in 1976 when I was driving cross-country with a friend. I was riding shotgun, watching one of the prairie states slip by when all of a sudden I *saw* a man being run over by a tractor. Now it wasn't "real time" seeing, but it seemed like it was happening outside my mind's eye. Very weird. And what was weirder was in that second, my friend asked, "What'd you just see?"

"What do you mean, what did I just see?" I asked, trying to size up his question.

"You just saw something; what did you just see?"

"Why? Did you see something?"

"Well . . . "

"Did you?"

"Well, yeah."

"So what did you just see?" I asked, determined not to be the first to share my "Gullible's Travels."

"Okay," he said. "I saw a man being run over by a tractor driven by his son."

"That's weird," I said.

"I know," he said.

"No, I mean — I saw it, too!"

As we drove over the plains we told each other what we'd seen and what we knew — the tale of the son, the father, and the mother who'd died giving birth.

To this day I don't know where it came from: Was it a memory the land held holographically? Was it a past life we'd shared? Or did the daydream of one of us become a telepathically received tale? I'll probably never know.

However this account was light-years away from my conscious

thoughts during that summer in Aspen. Why when I'd used the image seed of Nut's birth, had my unconscious dished up something so fabulously dissimilar? But look how interesting this is: the image that kept reminding itself to me worked like a mnemonic, and that's probably why Nut's birth haunted me. That image held within it a story that was mine to tell.

For many years I thought "Tractor " and the revisions I'd made on it were the story. But the image — now of the man being run over by the tractor driven by his son — kept haunting me. I knew it was time finally to find out why.

On March 1, 1988, I had just finished my story "The Soul of the Game." My daily record for that day includes this note about "Tractor ":

> I finished Soul, but the ending disturbs me . . . . It's like "Soviet Realism": nothing comes out well in the end. And it won't in Tractor either, which I'm already fleshing out in my head. (I'm excited about this project and can hardly wait for tomorrow to come.)

The next day, though, I didn't get to work on Tractor because money concerns intruded. I wrote my column for the local paper and "walked through snow balls the size of spit wads falling from a great thundering sky" to give it to my editor.

On March 3rd I wrote,

> This morning was great. On a lark, I started using a short story "Study Buddy" (step-by-step how-to) I've had since I taught fiction at College of DuPage. I'd bought it, but I'm not sure I ever read it. So I thought I'd use it to build the armature for Tractor. Didn't expect much, but it's amazing the outcome. A whole structure laid before me from beginning to end (with the beginning and end, too). And I know they're right. It's going to be a dynamite story.

And then I spent the rest of the day interviewing for a job.

On March 4:

> I worked on Tractor, developing who, what, . . . and transposing the original text to the appropriate scenes. I really

wonder, though, how much I will ultimately use. The original was telling and my style uses such a minimum of description these days. I'll find out because the next step is to start giving form to this clay that's on the armature. That's best done, I've found, in "timed" writings. Then the worst part, the neck muscle-bunching task of transposing onto the computer. This task is only bearable because it leads to the fun: the shaping (or in my new parlance, the directing).

By "timed" writings, I meant Natalie Goldberg's *Writing Down the Bones* style of writing. I'd been taking classes in this technique from a local Santa Fe poet, Miriam Sagan. She'd give us a topic — garter belts, for instance — and for a set amount of time, we'd write *en masse*, filling pages with whatever flowed off our pen — crossing out wasn't allowed. Then we'd read to the group who never critiqued, but only commented on what was "hot." It was fun, and the best part was the homework: we were supposed to meet other writers in restaurants, coffee shops, public places of all sorts and do these timed writings together. Although I'd done a lot of free writing over the years, including my own "immersion writing," I'd never had it be such a social event. Great play! And also great training. I discovered I could write just about anywhere — something I'd suspected during my year in a newsroom. And write anywhere I did. While my son was at his karate classes, I'd do timed writings in the midst of kids cooing and screaming at the moving sculptures of metal ostriches bobbing in the splashing fountain at the shopping mall's food area. No place daunted me. Any place was a riverbank where I could dig some clay!

On legal pads or in spiral notebooks, I'd write without any conscious thought. It was almost like automatic writing, and when I did it best — that is really *immersed* myself in what I was doing so that I lost all track of time — I'd often tap the well and have amazing jewels land right there in the middle of what would have seemed so much mud if I'd been operating from my tip-of-the-iceberg analytical thought mode. It's a priceless technique — one I still teach today — and to illustrate it here, I include some of the clay I dug while "Tractor" was making its metamorphosis to its final form.

My clay digging started at 8:30 A.M. on March 4th when I scribbled these words in a green spiral notebook:

> Tractor The tractor stands tall in the dream, as seen from a
> child's eyes and it stands, its engine a thrum and pulse and
> cat purr and the wheels a big rounding of rubber, grayed
> black and above is a boy who's almost a man.

It went on like that in a present tense account for a page, which ends
as Justice wakes and his newborn son is in his arms. Then I played
with the idea of his son closing his eyes, and, just as the world was
said to end if the Egyptian god Horus closed his eyes, Justice's world
would end with his son's eyes closing. That led to:

> Quite a dream. And earlier dreams? Prophecy. He dreams
> he's to marry her. Go to a dance and find her.

I only wrote two pages that morning, but I learned something that
would prove to be vital to the story.

That afternoon, I must have found some more time because I
wrote three more pages that started: *He returned home from the field,
the mud thick on his boots.* But like so much of this sort of writing, it
ended up being a "piss and moan" session for a couple paragraphs
— complaining about how I was feeling:

> In the morning, I often feel like I'm surfacing out of quick-
> sand. I want to be working on Tractor now. Not writing
> about this.

So after a page of "piss and moan," I started again — this time with
Justice talking. And oddly he wasn't as silent as I would have
guessed he would be. But he certainly was laconic:

> My name is Justice. I'm a God-fearing man. Never been
> married, but God told me in dream that it's time. And he
> picked my wife for me. I just have to travel to the farm . . .
> and there I'll find her.

He talks about going to find his bride, and finding a harvest cel-
ebration taking place in a barn: *I don't cotton to dancing.* He talks
some about that day, and then he tells me he was born to Joseph and
Sarah on the land he's living on.

On Saturday and Sunday, I didn't write at all, which I decided to make up for on Monday. My daily record for the 7th starts out: *Wrote from 8 to 3 pm longhand (39 pages).* Looking back over those thirty-nine pages, I can see the story taking shape. But I must not have known I was going to do a marathon because the spiral note-book entry starts *7:55 a.m.*

> Write for 15 minutes to just get the juices flowing, the camera rolling, the ball bearings greased. And in that dig-ging, How to get the syntax, the voice right? I can see him, hear his breath even, but he's so silent, so withholding of his voice. And more and more, I come back to this. This may be, as the original was, a silent story without dialogue . . . . What I like about this (original) story is that sparse tone that so matches the land (which is mythical — could be anywhere) and the character of Justice. I don't want to change that, and the way to preserve it is to keep it at that telling distance. Dialogue brings you too close. Like this for instance.
> 'Justice, please, couldn't you be more gentle.'
> 'How would you know about gentle?' And the sound of his slap echoed over the bare tree limbs.
> Rather than:
> He took her like he roped a calf for branding. She'd never had another, but she thought it could be different. She sug-gested it. He'd slapped her. That's when she learned to be silent.
> But the problem with this telling is that I've got it pre-marriage (in the rewrite). This then is when she runs from him. She won't have him. Realizes this is not the man she wants.

Before the first fifteen minutes of clay digging was up, a new (and disturbing) element of the story was already making itself known.

I scribbled more words, which led to another chronicling of his being at the dance and seeing the woman *he was after.* Most of it was, as most clay digging is, words I'd never use, but there in the midst of all the muck were some I liked: *Someone whispered that's Joseph's son . . . the word spread like _____ around the room.* (I often underline a blank space when just the right word won't come: leave it for the critic.)

At 8:30 A.M., I started my second fifteen-minute segment with

His father-to-be appeared on his door on Christmas day as he knew he would. He was delivering his daughter to Justice! What a weird bit of information that was for me. That was followed by an account of how they spent their winter and how in the spring he rode over to his father-in-law's to get the tractor. Instantly, I knew that was wrong: *No*, I wrote. *One day, his father-in-law appeared with a Tractor.* Another bit of important information uncovered — nothing I could have "thought to" either. Like the details about the pre-marriage sex and the delivery of the daughter, it surprised me when it came off my pen. But I knew it was *right* in that way we know these things are right: it resonated.

At 8:45 a.m., I started my third fifteen-minute stint with a piss and moan:

> Why is this THE hardest part of writing? Why would I much rather do anything than this? Yet this is where the dream is fleshed out, the clay added to the armature. I much prefer the modeling. The final touches. This is the part I must learn to love, though. Thank goodness for Miriam's classes which have taught me to write through the feelings of not wanting to write, having nothing to say. Back to the story.
> Tractor. The dream. It was like in the dream. It was just as the dream. It was kin to the dream . . .

A paragraph-long dump on the dream led to this:

> That dream [was] sent him like a command from God. That dream was God's command he knew. He acted on God's command the next day. Dressing in the one suit his father had left him. The one he hadn't been buried in, traveling though it might mean coming back on the Sabbath, though it meant missing a day clearing the silage from his fields. And he traveled East toward the place he'd seen in his dream. The place where God had showed him his wife would be.

I was starting to see the beginning of the story — what he did before he went to the dance to find her.

And again I chronicled the dance:

> Inside the barn, the folks were dancing on the raw plank floor, and the sawdust mixed with the smell of new mown hay.

And then there was a repeat of the whispers that it was Joseph's son, but the chronicling was getting richer:

> I do believe it's the son of old man Joseph who died last year. The old man with the visions, recall him? The whisper spread around the room like a prairie fire but Justice stood fixed in the doorway, his stocky body broad stanced . . .

Then at 9:25 A.M., I start the next burst with:

> The instant his eyes adjusted to the dim light of the barn, he saw her standing in a group, a gaggle, a crush, a flock, a covey of women . . .

Like most of the material that comes out in clay digging — useless — but in the midst of all that slush, a jewel:

> her hands holding an apple pie, the crust puffed high above the mounds below, the cover a pale brown, cinnamon dusted.

How rich in multiple meanings! I knew instantly it had to go in the story.

Justice talks to her father, but he's not so keen on the idea that God wants Justice to have his daughter. He says he'll wait until the Lord tells *him*. Nice stuff! But in the next fifteen minutes I voiced my worry that I'd gotten into dialogue!

> Course there's not too much more dialogue than this — not much possible because of the character and the story.

But fortunately that led me back to Justice's sparse world and this appeared under my pen:

> He sat at night by the light of an oil lamp, reading his Bible. It was his one extravagance. But this night he couldn't read. He just sat, the Bible on his denim-covered knees, the black leather cover stenciled with the words Holy Bible in gold. He sat holding the Book, listening for a sign, and his hand moved forward and parted the pages. They drop open with a fine crinkle of onion-thin paper to the Book of _____, and his finger fell to these words: a sign from the Lord; she

is with child. He knew then what he should do. He saddled up his horse and rode it through the night to her father's farm . . . .

The two pages that followed, were hard to write: Justice rapes this young woman.

The story had just taken a most ominous twist for me. I had suspected, but until I chronicled the scene, I hadn't wanted to see it.

After the description of the rape come these words:

> [I] Realize he opens the Book after he courts her. But her father won't acquiesce.

That's how I came to know that before the rape there was a period of courting. Then comes:

> He waited then in the patience of the Lord and on Christmas day when the ground was frozen, hard-packed dirt and snow swirled in wisps over the ground like God's breath, they came to the door.

Yes — I was starting to understand why this man had brought his daughter to Justice. All that took only a half an hour to write because the next entry's at 10:18 A.M. It's an account of cleaning and feeding and naming his child after the birth.

> As the mother's body grew cold on the bed and the night dropped like a fist tight-squeezed around them, Justice and the baby slept.

And again he dreams the dream that started the clay digging that first day — the dream of the tractor in the field, which ends this time

> the tractor rolling over his head like a wheel over a melon left too long in the field.
> Justice wakes. His wife is still cold in his bed, his child's weight is in his arms . . .

More of the story was making itself known.

At 10:40 A.M., I began again to chronicle their winter spent in his one-room shack, and I learned he read the Bible outloud as she sewed: . . . *she preferred [his] voice to the silence, the stories peopled her world with life.*

Then the clay digging jumps as it always does: Justice announces that her father's coming. She gets up from the bed and

> looked out the one window, staring toward the horizon where the sun hadn't yet appeared but whose light laid a line of gold, like a strand of straw-colored hair lit by fire-light.

I liked that image!

She makes breakfast, they eat, and two hours after sunrise, her father came *riding a tractor, a tied horse galloping behind.* But I knew there was something wrong here. At 11:17 a.m., I start with,

> The tractor. How does the tractor get there. It's a gift from her father. Why?

Trying to work that out by digging some more clay led to the realization that there's a car and a preacher, too! No horse. Just a preacher who's been brought along to consecrate their union. But, of course, Justice thinks it's not necessary because, as he says, *This child is God's Will.* But her father wins out and the preacher *marries them there on the stoop.* I chronicled the clothes that they wore and saw Justice's boots: *heavy dried leather boots with the tongues curled over the leather laces.*

What a detail — a fine-textured clay amidst all the mud. Then I chronicled the rains and spring plowing.

> As I write, the detail starts to flesh it out, make it richer . . . .
> The richness is in the details.

But I was worried about sustaining the reader's interest:

> There's so little action, and it's such a heavy story . . . a stern story . . . Justice. A prophetic man, harsh as the Old Testament, stern as the Old Testament God.

At 12:10 p.m., I was still at it. Again, dreams:

> It was as he dreamed it. The child was halfway out when the contractions stopped . . .

And, again, back to the barn, the dance and:

> Justice's face screwed in a displeased frown (who cares what he does. Why do we even care about this character? . . .)

I was getting fed up with Justice.

But I went on and chronicled the scene in the barn yet again, which led to this:

> Every Sunday through October he rode out to her father's house. He'd walk with her in her father's orchard, out to the big tree. He never talked and out of his silence, she created the man she'd always wanted.

My unconscious hadn't forgotten this gem from "Tractor"; as it always does, it fed it up from the well at just the right moment. In addition, it was showing me the courting and Justice's obstacle: *Still her father held firm, thought she could do better.*

So that's why he opened the Bible and let his finger fall. I chronicled the scene yet again:

> He took his Bible off the shelf and sat down on the bed. The book fell open before him and his dirt-creased finger fell to the page, he read, "_____."

The scene that preceded the rape was starting to make a horrible kind of sense.

On the next pages, I went back and forth — the rape, the courting, the Sunday spent in prayer when he opened his Bible, the rape again, Christmas day, the winter. By 1:15 P.M., I was in the fields again:

> The rains stopped and the sun came out as hot as a midsummer sun and dried the earth into a caking like crumbling plaster.

Justice walked out across the field and came back, his boots coated with dust on top, caked with mud on the bottom. It was almost time for the seed, he said as he turned from her to sleep.

The next morning, she rose before dawn and got the fire going and the biscuits rolled before he woke. He got up as he always did, in one movement, without stretching, and as he walked past her out the door to the privy, he said, "Your father's coming today."

I'd written it all before, but somehow in the intervening time, my unconscious had made it richer, fuller, more complete. The marathon was paying off in ways I could never have anticipated.

A little after 1:40 P.M., I must have started moving the good clay — the gems, the treasures, the porcelain-producing clay — to the computer because I find this note: . . .

transcribing from my notebook to the computer ranks even higher on the list of awfuls than [digging the clay]. [Clay digging] really isn't awful. Just exhausting, hard work. It'll come out a-ok, though.

When I came back to clay digging, the young woman finally broke through to tell some of the story. From her I learn her father's name: Hiram. I learn her mother died two years before, that she's sixteen, that she takes care of her younger siblings. I learn how she thinks she looks: *My hair's too black . . . . My face isn't that pretty.*

And then I hear her tell of meeting Justice, which culminates in an image I liked. She says his eyes *had an intensity . . . like a log firelicked.* I put a star next to that in the margin — I didn't want to risk not being able to find an image as good as that when it came time to transfer it to the computer.

By then it was 2:10 pm., and I was

Sipping hot chocolate, wondering if this marathon is really worth it. Wondering how much really comes out of this process — as opposed to the computer . . . . looking back over this day, I'd say aside from the thumb joint strain and the growing fatigue, it's been worthwhile. Material has come out I couldn't have thought. The writing's brought the scene to life in my mind — made it more real. I'm left with a question. Does Justice have any redeeming features? Let's ask him and see what he says . . .

— If you were god-fearing people, you'd know.

I ask him then why he seems so old. He launches into a tale that surprises me with its richness of detail — things like

I was raised by my father to do hard work from an early age. My mother left when i was young. Said it was no place for a woman. My father agreed.

It's in his telling the events of his life that I find out his family name is Barker. Oh, and here's a telling line!

I don't much care to delve into the past. If the good Lord would want us to be knowing, he would have given us the time to think.

We sure give ourselves away with our words — characters and humans alike!

At 2:30 p.m. I had a breakthrough:

GOD'S WILL for a title. Throughout: it's God's will. He named his son. He named his son Will as his father had named him Justice.

I ended the day where I started it: again the newborn and the dream of the tractor. And then a couple pages on, again I chronicled Justice waking to see his son's eyes — in the midst of which my unconscious finally provides a description of the eyes that I liked:

the whites like unseparated milk, the irises the blue of water after a rain.

In the last moments of the day's digging, I was still clinging to Horus: that the closing of Will's eyes would be the end of the world for Justice. The story had a different idea. *No. No. No. There's a neat nifty doodle ending in here somewhere* — after seven hours of writing, I was entitled to be a bit goofy —

Justice woke with a start. As he looked down at the sleeping baby in his arms, God's Will opened his eyes.

Ah, the meaning was making itself known! If the dream of the woman who would bear him a son was God's will, then the dream of Justice dying under the wheel of the tractor driven by his son must be God's Will as well.

All that in one day! What I wrote in my daily record hardly seems to touch the surface of the experience:

> Wrote from 8 to 3 longhand (39 pages). Came up with the title: God's Will. Ran into several problems — one is how much if any dialogue to use. It's a terse story (dry and nothing as the land). It's not really a problem because I know my answer. I just hope I won't bore my reader with the storytelling tone. I think it will be okay. Marathons, like today, are crucial for developing the story. I feel I'm building the "muscle" for them. That's followed by a note of panic the next day: I feel a bit of anxiety this morning (stage fright). It's released some when I tell myself I don't have to transcribe all 39 pages, but can start the modeling/shaping process. Then the excitement grows.

That night I wrote 10:10 P.M.

> I wrote well this morning, taking pieces from my notebook and working them into what I'd written already. I started getting into that real high I associate with this stage of the writing process (the shaping the dream — finding the right words to convey the dream in all its sense impressions). Unfortunately I had to stop by 11 . . .

In the next days, I worked on the computer, moving the clay around on the armature, trying to find the story's most beautiful form. Then on March 14th, I went back to digging the clay:

> Reading Lawrence Block's *Telling Lies for Fun and Profit* to get the juices flowing this Monday morning (maybe if I didn't take weekends off it wouldn't be like starting a frozen engine). One thing he says that struck me is write what you'd like to read, what would interest you. And I'm thinking with Tractor that what I'd like to read is a story about a fanatic that gets caught by his own structure-of-meaning. I like that; that's the way it is now. What I don't like about Tractor is that she's (Anne's) so undeveloped. She could be inter-

changeable (and maybe that's the point). I think I'll do some conversations with and between characters. Anne.

But as I wrote that name, I must have sensed something, for I asked if her name were really Anne. *No, she told me: Naomi.* All of a sudden, the story opened up for me in a way it hadn't before. Naomi and I talked and she told me she had another *beau who's been courting her,* but that she's interested in Justice because

> He's older — has a farm — is already established. And he wants me. I feel he's got a depth, unlike my younger suitor. Then also there's the fact that my father says no so fervently, so adamantly. I'm trying to understand why. He's so open to people, so giving, so caring, but all he'll say about Justice is what a zealot he is.

And then I asked her how she felt when he raped her.

> Like I'd done a terrible thing coming out to him like that, tempting him in my nightgown and robe. But I felt it was urgent or he wouldn't have come like that.

Then she described the rape and after it was over she said she

> bit my lips to keep from crying and he said . . . you're my wife now. And I knew it was true because of what my mother had told me before she died . . . . I kept wishing for my mother to be alive so I could run to her, but she was dead, three years buried. And my father wouldn't understand because he's been telling me I'm encouraging him. Don't encourage him, he says. But I didn't know he would do this. How could I? I had no idea. But it's my fault. I shouldn't have come out like I did. I shouldn't ever have encouraged him.

The story just seemed to get sadder and sadder. But finally I was beginning to know the all of it.

On the 17th I wrote in my spiral notebook: *I feel I'll finish today.* I was almost right. At the end of the day, I wrote in my daily record:

> Writing went very well. I finished the story except for the beginning and, maybe, the tractor dream.

My last day on the story was interesting. Bright and early on March 18th, I started in on the beginning, which was Justice's dream of the birth of his child — and his wife's death. But I just couldn't get it right. I finally pulled out my spiral notebook and did what I always do when I'm stuck: I wrote longhand, digging some more clay. The clay amounted to ten quickly written beginnings. I worked and worked and worked. Finally I went to take a bath — another thing I do when I'm stuck. Submerged in the water, it came to me. I didn't need the dream to start the story. I went dripping to the computer, slashed the first paragraph, and "God's Will" was done.

GOD'S WILL

Justice arose from his bed, pushed his feet into his cracked, dusty boots with the tongue curling toward the leather laces, and, without lighting the lamp, walked in his long johns to the shelf where he kept his Bible. Holding it in his hands, he fell to his knees and thanked God for his dream.

Then, although it was the Sabbath, he dressed in his best suit, saddled his horse, and rode east from his one room house, over his fields, toward the flat horizon, following the pictures the Lord had laid in his mind.

It was a good two hours before he came to the farm. He could hear the music from a ways off, a fiddling coming from the barn, the sound of feet stomping and laughter. He didn't take to music and would have turned around, but this too had been part of his dream. He rode to the side of the barn and tied his horse to the door handle of a Model T.

The big barn doors were closed against the cool of the early fall air, so he walked through the small door. Inside, folks were dancing on the raw plank floor and the smell of sawdust mixed with the dust from the new mown hay that filled the loft above. The fiddler's bow slid to a stop, eyes turned toward Justice, whispers stirred. The word spread like prairie fire from the ones who had a vague recollection who he might be to those who had not a clue: "I do believe it's the son of Joseph . . . Old man Joseph . . . the one what died last year. That strange old man what thought he saw the future."

Justice stood fixed in the doorway, his stocky body broad stanced, his hands open by his sides. With eyes charred like fire-licked logs, he searched through the dim light of the barn until he found her working among the women. Her eyes raised slowly to meet his, her hands, caught midair, held a pie, the pale brown crust puffed high above the mounds below, the cover cinnamon-dusted. In front of her food was piled on white tablecloth-covered planks laid cross saw horses. She smiled and dropped her eyes.

He stood transfixed. She wore the same blue calico he'd seen in his dream, and had the same black hair, but she wore it up, of course, instead of flowing as it had over the bed clothes. And her face, not sun-reddened and streaked with sweat, but fair. He knew it was she. The one God intended.

By the fiddle player stood a man, watching like all the rest. When Justice looked his way, he raised a stein of beer in a salute. Justice crossed the barn.

"Welcome to my home," said the older man thrusting his hand out for Justice to take. "My name is Hiram Oldenfeld. And you, young man, would be the son of Joseph Barker?"

"Justice be my name."

Hiram raised his pipe to his mouth. "What brings you out our way?"

"I come for your daughter," said Justice.

Some around Hiram laughed, but he sucked his pipe and studied Justice's eyes. "My Naomi's but sixteen."

Justice looked over to where she stood, watching, listening. Her eyes met his. "It is as the Lord intended," he said.

"Who put this notion into your head?" asked Hiram.

"God."

"God? God spoke to you?"

"He gave me a dream."

"A dream?"

"She is to bear me a son."

"You saw this in a dream?"

"Yes."

Hiram pulled a match stick from his coat pocket, struck it against a post, and lit his pipe. He pulled the smoke deep into his lungs, held it for a time, and released it in a thin stream. "No," he said finally. "God has not told me. We will wait until He does, shall we?"

"I will not defy the Lord," said Justice and turned on his heel. Laughter followed him out the barn door.

Every Sunday through the fall, Justice rode to Hiram's farm. He and Naomi would walk in the orchard that spread out in two directions from the white frame house. They'd walk among the trees, and she'd talk. She told him about her mother who had died nearly three years before, about her brothers who were married and her sister who lived with her husband in the big city that Naomi hoped one day to see. She talked of her two younger sisters and the brother still at home, and what a handful they were, but how much she loved them, and how she wanted children, many children, just like them. And she talked of her father as though he brought light to the earth.

Justice never spoke. He listened Sunday after Sunday while the autumn leaves danced around him to their death.

Then he'd ride home.

Naomi's father remained firm. He still hadn't heard from God, he said.

But Justice wooed Naomi, wooed her with his maleness, his strength, and his silence. She liked to imagine what he was feeling, and out of his silence, she created the man she'd always wanted. She'd have no other. Still her father said no.

Day after day, Justice prepared his farm for winter. Night after night, he sat and read his Bible by the light of his one oil lamp. In sleep, he looked to his dreams for answers, but he found none.

On the last Sunday in October, he rose as usual, but he didn't saddle his horse. Instead he spent the day on his knees.

Night fell early with the tight blackness of the new moon, and he finally stood and lit his lamp and took his Bible from the shelf. Then he sat on the edge of his bed, the Book on his denim-covered knees, the black leather cover embossed with gold. He sat holding the Bible, listening for a sign, and his hand moved forward and parted the pages. They dropped open with a fine crinkle of onion-thin paper. His black-lined finger fell to the page, and he read, "Therefore the Lord himself shall give you a sign; Behold, a virgin shall conceive, and bear a son, and shall call his name Immanuel."

He knew then what God would have him do. He saddled his horse and let the animal make its way through the dark to her house. There he stood by the window of the room where she slept with her sisters. He stood still, looking in, until his presence woke her. He'd lit a match so she could see him. He pointed to the orchard, turned, and walked away.

He was standing straight under the oldest tree when she came scrambling like a lamb over the fallen leaves. He grabbed her in the dark and parted her coat and lifted her nightgown up high to pull her pantalets down, but she twisted away from him and started to run back to her father's house. He caught her by the leg like he was roping a calf for branding, ripped her pantalets, and without removing his clothes, pulled his member free and thrust it into the space between her legs, thrust deep, ripping past the hymen, feeling the blood spill red and mix with his seed. She didn't cry out. Just bit her lip. But he could see her eyes, wild bright like an animal in the dark. He left her lying in the night.

He waited then, sure in the Lord, and on Christmas day they came. He could see them riding over the ice-packed ground on the buckboard, wisps of snow swirling like God's breath around them. Hiram pulled up in front of the house. They sat for a time, the two of them, on the buckboard. Justice stood at the door.

Hiram climbed down slowly. "She is yours now, I reckon," he said, but he didn't lift her down. Naomi sat still, hunched in the wagon, her eyes squeezed closed, her hands held tight-clasped within her muff.

Hiram went for the trunks, and Justice stepped forward to take Naomi from the wagon. She held back, and he grabbed her wrist tight until she looked into his eyes and allowed herself to be lifted onto his land.

"She is with child," said Hiram.

Justice didn't answer. He picked up a trunk on his shoulder and carried it through the door.

Hiram climbed back on the wagon. "I shall return in the spring when the preacher comes."

"No need," said Justice as he walked from the door and took his place beside Naomi.

"To make the child legitimate in the eyes of the Lord, man!"

"No need," said Justice. "He is God's will."

Hiram turned the horses and flipped the reins to get them moving. Naomi started to run after him, but Justice grabbed her by the arm. "Pa," she cried. "Pa!"

Hiram rode away without turning back.

They sat, the two of them, through the winter, the wind lashing the North side of the house, the snow piling up. Naomi would sit on the bed sewing or mending, and Justice would sit, as he'd done every winter, in the hard-backed chair at the square table, his Bible open before him, reading aloud. Because she hadn't come until Christmas, he'd begun again. She listened avidly. The stories peopled her otherwise silent world.

With spring, the rains came in torrents and washed the fields into the muddy river that overflowed, flooding his lower fields, washing away the topsoil. Then the rain stopped, and the sun came out as hot as a midsummer sun and dried the earth into a caking like crumbling plaster.

Justice walked out across the field and came back with his boots coated with dust on top, caked with mud on the bottom.

"It is time for the plowing," was all he said.

The next morning, Naomi got up from the bed before dawn and got the fire going. It turned to coals as she made up the biscuits and put them into the oven to bake. She put drippings in the cast iron skillet and laid in a slice of ham. When the ham was crackling, she broke the one egg and dropped it into the grease. The sizzling woke him. He got up as he always did, in one movement, without stretching. "Your father's coming today," he said, as he walked past her, out the door to the privy.

She looked out toward the East where the sun hadn't yet appeared, but had laid a line of gold, like a strand of straw-colored hair lit by firelight, along the flat horizon.

While he ate his food at the table, she stood by the warm stove and dipped yesterday's biscuits into the drippings.

Two hours after the sun came up, they saw dust rising like smoke on the horizon. Naomi stopped her work and put on her best, a loose-fitting gown stitched together from the dress she'd worn the day she first saw Justice. She coiled her braids over her head.

From the window, they could now make out a tractor pulling a plow followed by a Model T. Justice put up the harness he was mending, cleaned his hands, and put on his one white shirt, tucking it under the bib of his overhauls.

When the vehicles pulled up in the yard, Naomi ran out the door. "Pa!" she called as she ran toward the tractor. "Pa!" The cold spring wind slapped her words away, whipped the calico sack over the small mound of her belly.

A preacher stepped out of the car. "I come to marry you, child," he said. His black cloth coat flapped in the wind.

She ignored him and threw herself at her father as he stepped to the ground. "Daughter," he said and kissed her on the cheek. "We come to get you wed."

"Come over here," said the preacher. He arranged Naomi next to Justice, and Hiram next to him. Then holding his broad-brimmed hat with one hand and his Bible in the other, he married them there on the stoop.

When it was over, Hiram kissed his daughter and walked quickly toward the car. He opened the door and was getting in when he turned and said, "This tractor. It's for you."

He climbed in the car, the preacher turned the engine over, and they drove away.

Justice walked slowly toward the tractor. He stood looking for a time, walking around it, examining the motor, the tires. Then he climbed up and sat on the perforated metal seat, pumped the pedals, curled his hands over the black rubber wheel, letting his fingers settle into the knuckle grooves on back. He sat like that for a long time, and finally he looked down to where Naomi stood on the stoop. For the first time since she'd known him, he smiled.

The baby was born in June. Naomi was in the field when the contractions started. She worked on, crawling along the earth, pulling weeds, her full belly dragging the ground.

By evening, the pains came sharper, closer together. She got him his supper before she took to bed.

Through the night, her contractions ripped her body. He tried to lie beside her, but she would go rigid with the pain and wake him. He rose finally and sat at the table, his finger tracing along the lines as he read in the faint light from the lamp.

Her pains came fast, one on top of the other, faster and faster. "Help me," she screamed. "Help me!"

He didn't answer, just sat reading.

Another pain wrenched her body, and she arced back, her mouth a wide-open, silent cry that went on and on. Then she collapsed, panting, whispering, "Help me. Please."

Justice read on. He read aloud, reading louder to cover her noise. "For whatsoever a man soweth, that shall he also reap."

"A monster you will reap," she whispered from the bed.

He turned his head slowly toward her, his eyes widening.

"I curse you," she said, snuffling like an animal, her fingers digging at the bedclothes, her back stretching and stretching up and toward the ceiling. Then she fell, back onto the bed, her mouth open, but silent, her body still.

He went to her then, and he knew she was dead. He pulled the covers back and lifted the nightdress up over her full belly. By the thin light of the lamp, he saw a glistening head breaking past her mounds now flattened, a forehead, eyes squeezed shut, a nose.

He dug then, dug with his hands, up into that slippery, cooling space, and pulled the child out. He pulled gently as his man's hands would let him, but there was a suction that pulled the child back in. The child was crying already, and that was good — he wouldn't have to clean him out. It took a mighty thrust and pull, but finally he got the child out. He left the afterbirth in her. He had no roses to feed.

He cleaned his son and wrapped him in a swaddling blanket she'd made from one of her nightgowns, and he set him to suck at his dead mother's breast while he went out to milk the goat. He fashioned a teat from an old bit of cloth as he'd done for the animals that'd lost their mum.

The child was crying when he returned. He drew him from his mother's embrace and held him in his arms, sat in the high-backed chair. He held the teat, and the boy sucked. Justice looked deep into the eyes of his son, the whites like unseparated milk, the irises the blue of water after a rain. He named the boy Will as his father had named him Justice. "You are God's Will," he said to his son.

As the mother's body grew cold on the bed and the night dropped like a fist tight-squeezed around a dying bird, Justice and Will slept.

And Justice dreamt.

He dreamt that the sun was setting like a purple slash against the sky and from the horizon he could hear a sound like the roar of a thousand locusts. The sound grew and the shape of his tractor became visible against the sunset. He ran over the furrows his wife had weeded, tripping over the dry ground that had no shoots. The roar of the tractor grew, but he couldn't see who sat on his seat, who pressed the accelerator pedal, who ground the gears. He ran closer, but the shape was a shadow, black against the setting sun.

Justice ran around the tractor and looked up into a face, a young man's face, and he saw his own face, and he saw his wife's. Justice's eyes found the young man's, and they were his wife's, wild like an animal in the night. Justice knew he was looking into the eyes of his son. He heard the gears grate and saw the tractor begin to roll. He stood, watching his son's eyes, watching as the tractor knocked him over, as the big wheel crushed his chest and pushed him back into the soft cushion of dust, as the tractor rolled over his head like a wheel over a melon left too long in the field.

And just as the darkness swallowed him, he woke.

He sat in his chair, his wife dead on the bed, his Bible open on the table, and his son in his arms.

Imagine being in that guy's body for two weeks! Usually walking a mile in somebody else's shoes isn't such grueling work, but Justice was as arid and austere as that land. In some ways, this was the hardest story I've ever written.

And as you saw, digging the clay wasn't always easy either. It told me things I'd rather not have known; in fact, it told me things that without digging the clay I couldn't have known — that Justice was led to his wife-to-be through a dream, that he raped her to do what he felt was "God's will," that his dream of the tractor rolling over him if he interpreted it within the same structure of meaning, had to be showing him "God's will" as well. Digging the clay uncovered the real story — the meaning level — where "Tractor" had only told the "true story" — all the facts.

Clay digging also gave me the fullness of the story — the details that are so crucial to evoking the dream in our reader; the rhythm of the words that set the story's tone and thus impart atmosphere; the character's histories without which no story can ever be fully realized.

More than anything, though, all of this clay digging made the movies in my mind extraordinarily vivid. That, in itself, is essential for producing something in the minds of our reader they'll never quite be able to forget. And isn't that one of our goals as writers: to haunt for a lifetime?

DISCOVERING YOUR STORY

I want you to find the story that wants to be told by *you*. We all have stories that want us to tell them, but usually we don't pay attention to their yammering. Pay attention: just the act of making ourselves receptive lets our stories announce themselves to us. And announce themselves they do: We might be driving down the road and all of a sudden one will spring to mind; we might wake from a dream with an image seed; or we might be leafing through a magazine and see a picture that wrenches our heart. One of the richest veins for stories, though, is method writing. Just keep chronicling the movies in the mind, writing what you see, hear, taste, touch, smell, and feel until you get a sense of that incident that holds a story screaming to be told.

TIPS FOR CLAY DIGGING

1) Be willing to write without censoring *anything*. Just let it come off your pen. You'll be surprised by what surfaces. But don't let the surprises scare you.

2) Don't worry about the order of your clay digging. Be willing to chronicle whatever comes up. Jump around with great abandon. It's that sort of seeming randomness that takes us most out of our analytical minds and lets the storymaker start speaking.

3) Don't hold too tight to what you've written. Writing from the inside out is a fluid process; we have to be flexible enough to accept the changes that clay digging always produces.

4) Ask a lot of questions of your characters. It's easy if you're someone like me who loved being a journalist because it was license to pry. But if you're timid about such things, now's the time to get over it. Ask away! Your characters can only refuse to answer. Then ask the other characters to tell you about the one who won't talk. And don't limit it to the characters who'll appear in your stories. Ask anyone in any way associated with your characters — the long-dead mother, for instance. This is a realm where ghosts certainly do speak.

5) Don't make up biographies for your character. Let them tell you. They know their names (real and aka's), their histories, their dreams and goals. Write down your question; then write down your character's answer. And never take your character's answers at surface value: Our characters are no less complicated than we are. It's worth asking the question several times in the course of different conversations to get the answer's full dimension.

6) And don't just rely on what your characters tell you. Sometimes they lie; sometimes they don't know. Just as in real life, actions speak louder than words. We are what we do: if you want to know a person, you watch what they do — and it's the same with your characters. Watch your characters and record *everything* they do and the way that they do it. You never know what bit of clay will come in handy. I've always had students check to see how many pillows their characters slept on for when I was clay digging for *Dream Warriors,* I discovered my protagonist slept on twenty! That, I thought, was a pretty neat (and telling) detail. I started the book like this:

> Daphne Fey settled in for the night, fluffing her twenty pillows, arranging them like clouds around her on the oversized four-poster bed, pulling the chenille coverlet up tight under her fiercely double chin. She tugged the chain on the bedside lamp and tucked deep into the feather mattress she'd had for sixty years, since preadolescence. She'd been big even then.

Chronicling brings up great details.

7) Go beyond the situation of the story. Put your characters into situations that would be unusual for them just so you can see how they respond. You'll learn much more about them then you can if you just see them *in situ,* where their habits and the imprint of the expectations of others strip them of some of the range of their personalities.

8) Get inside the body of at least one of your characters. Write down what the world is like from inside: let your character taste, touch, smell things so that you can do it from inside their body. Go and look into a mirror. See what it looks like if you're just looking through the person's eyes as though you're actually you inside the

body versus you looking through their eyes at themselves in the mirror. Do both — go back and forth doing both — and see what the difference is. The world becomes a very different place if you can get inside another body.

9) And, most important, always let your character tell you the story. One of the biggest mistakes we writers make is in thinking *we* have to come up with a story. In fact, all we have to do is listen to our characters. In digging the clay, I've frequently discovered that they often knew better than I the best direction for the story to go.

CHAPTER FIVE

WHOSE STORY IS IT ANYWAY?

Remember Aristotle's axiom? He said "the pleasure the poet is to provide is that which comes from pity and fear." Fiction's needs are more diluted than drama in Aristotle's time, but pity and terror still make a good shorthand for what it takes to create an emotionally powerful story.

But how do we produce even a dilute version of pity and terror in our readers? It seems a weighty task, but it's really quite easy to achieve.

CONTINUUM TRAIT AND DELIMMA

Pull out your notebook right now. In it, you're going to be digging some more clay, but this time in the form of a question and answer session with your characters. As you ask each of the questions, you'll need not just to record your characters' answers but also their actions. What is your character doing as you ask the question? As they answer or don't answer? Write it all down — and not just their words and actions, but your words and any pertinent actions, too.

First write this question in your notebook: *What do you want?* It's your first question of your character. What does he or she say and do in response? As with each question you'll be asking, make sure you chronicle the responses as vividly as you can.

Just like us, characters always want something. Story grows out of what our characters do to meet their needs. Justice wanted to do God's will. Every scene in the story is about his doing just that — what he thought was God's will.

The second question to write down is, *Who or what is standing in your way?* First copy that question into your notebook, and then record your character's answer and actions.

In fiction just as in real life, anytime we want something, there's usually someone or something that'll make it hard.

Once you know these two things about your character, it's time to ask a couple more questions: *What's your greatest strength? and What gets you into the most trouble?* It doesn't matter which question you ask first, but make sure you ask both of them.

Frequently, a character will answer one, but not the other. For instance, I have a con man in one of my stories, and when I asked him what got him into the most trouble, he laughed and said, "Nothing. Nothing gets me in trouble." When I asked him his greatest strength, he answered, "I can talk anybody into any-thing." Easy to guess what also gets him into the most trouble.

The answer to these two questions typically points to the same trait because just as with you and me, what gets a character in trouble is usually that character's greatest strength. Think of the reports your grade-school teachers sent home. What did those who liked you say? What about those who weren't quite so crazy about you? The teachers who liked me commented positively on how "determined" I was; the teachers who weren't such fans called me "bullheaded." Both are aspects of the same trait that's rewarded and plagued me all my life: tenacity. But my teachers labeled that trait with a positive or negative emphasis, depending on how they felt about me. That's why I call this trait a *Continuum Trait*: It has both its good and bad sides; it's both our greatest strength and, when taken to extremes, the thing that gets us in the most trouble. Think of a Continuum Trait as a number line:

-1   0   +1

On the positive side of my number line, I'd write "determined" or some other positive adjective my friends might use to describe me (e.g., dedicated, committed, resolute). On the negative side of the number line, I'd write the "bullheaded" label or one of the negative adjectives my enemies might use to describe me (e.g., stubborn, obstinate, relentless). In the middle, I'd put "tenacious" because it's a word that's as close to value neutral as possible — one that carries neither a negative nor a positive connotation. It's not necessarily good or bad to be tenacious: it's just an is. My number line might look something like this:

bullheaded   tenacious   determined

-1   0   +1

A shorthand for my Continuum Trait then would be the word tenacious.

How does a character's Continuum Trait work in a story? The best example I've ever found is Sophocles' *Oedipus Rex*.

Sophocles used an old, well-known story as the base of his play: Oedipus' parents learned by way of an oracle that their baby was destined to grow up to murder his father and marry his mother. Needless to say, they weren't too keen on being a party to this denouement. They ordered one of their shepherds to take the baby to Mt. Kithairon, where with his feet pinned together, he was to be left to die. (Oedipus means swollen foot in Greek.)

The shepherd, however, took pity on the child. He handed him over to a shepherd from the other side of the mountain, who took him to his town of Corinth and presented him to the childless king and queen. They raised Oedipus as their own.

When he grew to manhood, Oedipus, too, learned of the prophecy, and he decided he'd have no part of it. He left Corinth behind to spare the couple whom he thought to be his father and his mother.

On the road, he encountered an old man in a chariot who wouldn't let him pass and who hit him with a stick. This riled Oedipus, and he pushed the man out of his way, killing him. Oedipus then continued on to Thebes, where he discovered the town nearly destroyed by the plague. To lift the plague, the Sphinx required an answer to her riddle of what went on two feet, on four, and on three but had only one name and when he goes on the most limbs, he's weakest.

Oedipus knew the right answer: Man. As a baby we go on all fours, crawling; in our prime, we walk erect; and in old age, we often rely on a third appendage — a cane.

Oedipus' answer lifted the plague, and as reward, he was made king of the Thebans and given their widowed queen as his wife.

Years later and on the day that Sophocles' play takes place, Oedipus learns that the old man on the road was his birth-father, and his wife, his birth-mother. In trying to beat the fates at their own game, he'd fallen right into their hands.

In his notes to his translation of Aristotle's *Poetics*, James Hutton wrote,

> Oedipus' hamartia or mistake is the slaying of a man who might be his father but whose relationship to himself he does not know, and this after warning from the oracle that he was destined to slay his father. This mistake might seem incredible had not Sophocles provided Oedipus with the hasty and irascible temper that makes it probable that he would act thus in circumstances of extreme provocation.

But Hutton was only looking at the surface. It isn't Oedipus' temper that got him into trouble: it's the Continuum Trait out of which that temper grew, a Continuum Trait Oedipus exhibited when he thumbed his nose at the gods and left his "hometown." Oedipus would bow to none: not to fate, and certainly not to a contentious old man on the road.

It should be easy to see, however, that what brings about Oedipus' downfall also brought him his successes. He was the sort of man whose friends might have said "he knows his worth" or "he bows to none." His enemies might have said "he heeds none" or "he thinks himself greater than the gods." And his number line in today's parlance might look like this:

cocksure	self-confident	assured
-1	0	+1

In short, his Continuum Trait is the stuff of kings. And all of Oedipus' actions in Oedipus Rex grow out of this Continuum Trait. Thus he brings about his own downfall not merely by a tragic flaw, but by being exactly who he is: a man who would bow to none. Likewise, all of my actions will grow out of my Continuum Trait: We do what we are. I know: I wouldn't have this flattened forehead if it weren't for all the brick walls my tenacity has brought me up against.

But Continuum Trait alone does not a story make. We need our readers to be sufficiently engaged in our character's plight to continue the story to its end. Here the key is dilemma — but not any dilemma: it must grow out of the character's Continuum Trait, which it will do automatically if we let our characters tell us their stories.

Take for example Mabel. Mabel is a woman in her sixties, a woman who collects things. She collects newspapers, magazines, string. Imagine her sitting in her chair in her living room, surrounded by stacks of newspapers. Why does she do this? Many reasons may come to mind, but in writing from the inside out, the source is always the character: Ask Mabel.

— Mabel, what's your greatest strength?

— I don't know, really. I'm not sure I have any, really.

— Well, what gets you into the most trouble?

— [She laughs.] Collecting things, I guess.

— Why do you collect things?

— Oh, just to be safe. You never know when you'll need a bit of string.

Although she hasn't said much, she's given a wealth of information. What does she want? She's told us: to be safe. A need for security of some sort motivates her. And what's her Continuum Trait? It's easy to imagine her friends calling her things like "provident" and "thrifty," but those who didn't like her would probably call her a "pack rat" or worse. But what's a "value neutral" word for her Continuum Trait? "Frugal" seems a good one. Her number line would look like this:

pack rat	frugal	thrifty
-1	0	+1

So, now we know Mabel's Continuum Trait: she's frugal; and we know what she wants: to be safe and secure.

As we've seen, art resembles life: Anytime we want something, there's always someone or something ready to stand in our way.

Enter Sam, Mabel's husband. He stops by the door, not even attempting to navigate the maze of newspapers stacked floor to ceiling. Sam sees Mabel sitting with her arm on a stack of magazines, rolling string around the huge ball in her lap. Since this is, after all, a story, what does Sam say? Right: he'll throw down the gauntlet — "Mabel, I can't take it anymore; either these things go, or I go."

When I use this example in classes or workshops, I have the participants experience it in their mind's eye as though they were reading it in a book. When I say Sam's words, their faces show pain, some even fold their arms across their bellies. Mabel's cluttered room might have sparked curiosity in them; evidence of her "frugality" might have made them interested. But when Sam delivers his ultimatum, they become engaged. It's a good illustration of the power of a dilemma that grows out of a Continuum Trait: it makes the reader care. This is one way we satisfy Aristotle's requirement that "the pleasure the poet is to provide is that which comes from pity and fear." This is what pity means in the context of a short story.

In a good story, we care about the characters. Unfortunately, too many people take that to mean that characters must be likable. Not so. Much of the world's great literature is peopled with men and women who aren't very endearing. Take a look at Hemingway's stories and see how many of his characters you'd actually like as friends. No, for a story to be good, readers don't have to like our character or even respect him or her, but they have to feel engaged by the character's plight to continue the story to the end. Here the key is dilemma — but not any dilemma: it must grow out of the character's Continuum Trait, which it will do automatically if we let our characters tell us their stories.

And Mabel's got a dilemma. Not the watered-down "dilemma" of the weakening of this word's meaning. No, this is no mere quandary. This is a "damned if you do / damned if you don't," right "on the horns of the bull" dilemma. If she gives up either her collection or her husband, she gives up something she needs.

But consider June: June loves to travel. All her forty years of adult life, she's been on the move, and as she went from country to country, she collected curios and knickknacks. Now, imagine June in her living room, surrounded by her collection. June's husband Harvey comes into the room and says, "Look, June, either these go or I go." What does June say? Right: "What's stopping you?"

Because June's collecting doesn't tie to her Continuum Trait, no dilemma's created when she's asked to choose. (Ask her, however, to choose between a travel-averse husband whom she loves and a continuing life of travel, and we may have another story.)

Mabel's dilemma is clear: she must give up all that she's collected as a hedge against uncertainty or she must resign herself to losing her husband. Both threaten her security: damned if she does, damned if she doesn't. Either way she can't win.

Once you know your character's dilemma, you can follow the "what?" to the story's end: "What's this character going to do to resolve this dilemma?" Mabel, for instance, may call the Lion's Club to come and get the newspapers, but as they're loading the truck, she might be extracting those she still hasn't read. She'll store these in the pantry because Sam never cooks.

"Did you get rid of that stuff today?" he'll ask.

"The newspapers," she'll say.

"They're gone?"

She'll cross her fingers behind her back because it'll be the first time since she was a child that she's lied, and she'll say, "Yes."

Then to show his appreciation the next day, he'll decide to do something he hasn't done since they were first married — make her breakfast in bed. He'll open the pantry door, and a stack of newspapers will fall out. So instead of breakfast in bed, she'll wake to his packing a suitcase . . . .

And it goes on from there.

That's the terror of Aristotle's requirement. In fiction, terror is just a dramatic word for that question that pulls us through to the end: "What?" That's the suspense of the story. We want to know the what of it — what's going to happen, what's the character going to do to get out of his mess, what's it all about anyway? In literary stories the question is more often "why?" The best literary writing, however, combines the two questions. And that suspense that the "what?" or "why?" proves is terror in the context of a story.

Your main character makes choices that bring him or her to the win or the lose or the draw of her story's conclusion. The discomfort of being in a dilemma will force those choices, but like Oedipus, your characters are not victims. They, too, operate from their Continuum Traits and, concomitantly, from their needs. Their needs, their Continuum Trait, their dilemma: they're all connected. Your characters do what they are — just like us. And only they can tell us that story.

DIALOGUE

Five questions: What do you want? Who or what is standing in your way? What is your greatest strength? What gets you into the most trouble? What are you going to do to resolve the dilemma?

Dialogue with your character, asking these questions in several different ways — and asking other questions. Talk to your characters, and let them talk to you. This is the time to listen and to get it all down.

CHAPTER SIX

UNLOCKING YOUR STORY

In the summer of 1988, I was listening to National Public Radio's "All Things Considered" as I made dinner. I'd just come in from lighting the charcoal when I heard someone say he'd had a lot of trouble writing his book until he got the voice right. It took me a few beats to realize I was listening to E.L. Doctorow talking about his new novel, *Billy Bathgate.*

Doctorow, as I recall, went on to say he'd known the story, but until he heard the voice of the young boy who tells the tale, he couldn't get the book to flow. Here's the first sentence of *Billy Bathgate*:

> He had to have planned it because when we drove onto the dock the boat was there and the engine was running and you could see the water churning up phosphorescence in the river, which was the only light there was because there was no moon, nor no electric light either in the shack where the dockmaster should have been sitting, nor on the boat itself, and certainly not from the car, yet everyone knew where everything was, and when the big Packard came down the ramp Mickey the driver braked it so that the wheels hardly rattled the boards, and when he pulled up alongside the gangway the doors were already open and they hustled Bo and the girl upside before they even made a shadow in all that darkness.

In that breathless rush of a first sentence, more than a character is born. A whole story can swoop from the right voice, laying itself down so fast that at times we can hardly write or type fast enough.

That's what happened for me with *Perchance to Dream.* It took weeks to get the voice even though I had an idea of the story. It bugged me through a move from Durango to Santa Fe. Finally it came while I took a break from unpacking and sat digging some clay in the warm Santa Fe sun:

> "Bergie. For God's sake, what is this shit? Listen to this. Are you there, Bergie? The headline in the Minneapolis Star reads 'Woman Found Levitating in SW Desert, Body Smells Like Roses.' My God Bergie. Is that you. Bergie come home! You're too old to do things like this. What will your grandkids say?"

Right after those words circled on that page in my spiral notebook, I wrote:

> I write this and tap a vein. I feel the chuckles spilling out. I want to play on this edge between absurd and business as usual. This is the point that's a line: this is whimsy. I love whimsy! I want it to color the whole book. As soon as serious intervenes, I want to reassert the whimsy.

I had found the voice! That circled paragraph captured it so well for me that with only minor changes, it became the opening of my book:

> "Bergie, for God's sake! What is this? Listen to this. Are you there, Bergie? The headline in the Minneapolis Star reads, 'Woman Found Levitating in SW Desert, Body Smells Like Roses.' My God, Bergie! Is that you. Bergie, come home. You're too old to being doing things like this. What will your grandkids say?"

Like Doctorow, once I got the voice, I couldn't stop the story. It just poured out of me. Before I got all the boxes unpacked, the book was well underway. And even though in the next six months I dealt with major personal trauma, served as president of a local press women's organization, bought a house, got married, moved again, mothered my sixteen-year-old, *and* taught three sections of English composition at the University of New Mexico (an hour drive from my home) the story kept me coming back to my computer. There was no stopping it.

And it was probably the same for Doctorow. When you know the voice of anything you're writing, whether it's fiction or nonfiction, it's like tumblers clicking into place. All of a sudden, the story starts telling itself — often with an alacrity that can, at times, feel overwhelming. You just have to write fast enough to keep up with it. In this chapter, I'm going to introduce you to some information that will help you find the voice to unlock your story.

But first of all, what is this thing we call voice? My most current dictionary — a 1989 release of the *Merriam-Webster* paperback — doesn't define voice in any way that's similar to how it's used by writers and editors today. The closest is "a sound suggesting vocal utterance." Does that mean that to have voice a story must be either in the oral sounds of a character's telling as in *Billy Bathgate* or of a conversation recorded as in the excerpt from my book? That would certainly limit what story is.

My Norton's second edition of *Writing: A College Handbook* defines voice as "The aspect of a verb that indicates whether the subject acts or is acted upon." That's to say: "Hank stole the car" (active voice) versus "The car was stolen" (passive voice). In the latter, there's no agency — no one to blame: thus the passive voice's popularity in the ever-burgeoning files of bureaucracy. No *one* buys $400 hammers for the military; they are bought.

As a writing teacher, I've been as guilty as any other writing teacher of making canon out of the active voice. It's true that active voice can make writing much livelier, but emphasis on it rang the death knell for a style of writing that has much to commend it. Norton's example of the passive voice — "The boat was rammed by the whale" — creates a mysterious atmosphere that the active voice example — "The whale rammed the boat" — lacks.

It might be this active voice fever that led to our current preoccupation with "voice." Maybe the word "active" just got dropped somewhere along the line. But the way writers and editors use it, voice means something more than lively writing.

Voice is like going into a museum and looking across the room and knowing that it's a Van Gogh on the opposite wall. His work has a signature that is recognizable from a distance. And so it is with some writers: if you were given five quotations from stories and told to assign one of five author's names to each, you could probably do it if the authors were Ernest Hemingway, Flannery O'Connor, Raymond Carver, Miguel de Cervantes, and William Faulkner. Not all writer's signatures are so bold; but each of us has a style, nonetheless. "Stop thinking about writing style as an outer garment with which to dress your thoughts," wrote William Safire in his *The New York Times Magazine* column in 1986.

> Style, in the sense I have in mind, is not the synonym of 'form,' the antonym of 'substance,' a fashion to be adopted and set aside. Style is not a mask, an image or a persona: upon his admission to the French Academy in 1753, Comte Georges-Louis de Leclerc Buffon said, "Style is the man himself," arguing that style is essence. The way you write reflects the way you think, and the way you think is the mark of the kind of person you are.

And he goes on to add that when he was talking about his own style in this column,

> What I really meant was more profound than "That's not the way I write"; it was also "that's not how I think," and when you keep peeling that onion until you're down where the tears are, "that is not the sort of person I am."

Style isn't something you get: It's something you already have. It's the self coming forth. And, paradoxically, that's one of the things that happens when we writers get out of our own way and let our stories tell themselves: Our writing takes on our own stamp.

This thing I call signature is not just "the kind of person you are." It is the intersection between "the man himself" and his or her craft. Rudolf Nureyev's ability to leap came from working hard at perfecting his technique. And yet it's those leaps that gave him something akin to a personal voice when he was on stage.

There are very few writers whose work we can pick up and say, "Oh, that's a Hemingway." Most of us write in a voice that will be different depending on what we're writing. If, for instance, I were writing a detective novel, I'd write it in a different voice than if I were writing a literary short story because I'm very aware of the stylistic differences between them. (Genres have personalities, too.) I like playing with voice in that way — the tone, the atmosphere, the mood — and yet I do see my style in all I write. There's a preoccupation with certain themes, a use of simile, and often a wryness of tone that marks my work.

So what is this thing called voice? There's another definition in my *Merriam-Webster* that I keep coming back to: "musical sounds produced by the vocal cords : the power to produce such sound." That brings us back to making our stories sing. Does saying a story has voice mean it sings? I like that. Maybe that's what makes the story take off by itself: we hit the right notes.

How confusing is this thing we call voice. And it's all the more confusing in this "Age of Voice" when editors reject a writer's work because "it lacks a strong voice." So, of course, writers want to know what voice is. It makes me think of the Zen koan, "What is the sound of one hand clapping." I heard it one day: that brilliance of silence. It's the same with voice: Whether or not we can name it, we know it when it's there. The right voice unlocks our story.

Your story's voice will depend on several choices you make: Who tells the story? At what distance? With what knowledge? Although these three things interweave inextricably in a story, I'm going to do what all writing teachers do — try to explain them as separate pieces.

First: Who tells your story? This is largely a choice of "person." Remember this from school? First person, second person, third person?

First person: I walked to the store, and on the way, I tripped over the curb and skinned my knee.

Second person: You walked to the store, and on the way, you tripped over the curb and skinned your knee.

Third person: He walked to the store, and on the way, he tripped over the curb and skinned his knee. She walked to the store, and on the way, she tripped over the curb and skinned her knee. They walked to the store, and on the way, they all tripped over the same curb and skinned their knees.

Do you see how your location as reader shifts with each example? If you're reading a story where a character acts as the narrator — "I walked to the store" — there's a sense of being close to that character. But when the narrator exists outside the story — "She walked to the store" — there's a greater sense of distance between you and the character. That's the power of this choice: it lets you determine how close you bring your reader to your characters.

Right now, first-person stories are popular, but it's not always the right choice for your story. Close is not always best. Some stories need a buffer zone to keep the reader reading. As Rita Mae Brown said in *Starting from Scratch*: "The reader doesn't want to get hurt, yet you want that reader to identify with your characters and that means to feel their pain and their joy."

To do that, the person we choose for the story must bring the reader in only as close as is comfortable. Imagine, for instance, if "God's Will" had been written in first person. At what point would you have stopped reading? Not all stories can (or should) be written in first person.

Because first person does create a sense of being close to the character, a good technique when you want a sense of distance in a story but still want the intimacy of the first-person voice is to write in first person and shift it later to the third. I'll use an example from Donald Barthelme's short story "Some of Us Had Been Threatening Our Friend Colby." Here are the first lines of the story:

> Some of us had been threatening our friend Colby for a long time, because of the way he had been behaving. And now he'd gone too far, so we decided to hang him. Colby argued that just because he had gone too far (he did not deny that he had gone too far) did not mean that he should be subjected to hanging. Going too far, he said, was something everybody did sometimes. We didn't pay much attention to this argument. We asked him what sort of music he would like played at the hanging.

Now if I change the pronouns to third person, it reads like this:

> Some of them had been threatening their friend Colby for a long time, because of the way he had been behaving. And now he'd gone too far, so they decided to hang him. Colby

argued that just because he had gone too far (he did not deny that he had gone too far) did not mean that he should be subjected to hanging. Going too far, he said, was something everybody did sometimes. They didn't pay much attention to this argument. They asked him what sort of music he would like played at the hanging.

Do you see how the intimacy is retained even though the pronouns change? The choice of person determines the way we as authors capture the fictional world. Changing the person after a piece is written gives it a certain skewed quality that readers can't quite put a finger on. It can make for provocative writing.

There's an interesting paradox, though, with first-person accounts. As much as they draw us in, making us feel close to the subject, it's usually the kind of closeness we feel with "others" in our day-to-day life. There may be an intimacy, but we are not they. For all its distance, third person can allow us to identify more closely with the characters, feeling more deeply their plight than we can with stories told in the first person. With first person, we may have curiosity, but with third person we are often taken inside the character. The closeness of first person is often a false intimacy because it's intimacy with a skin around it. Identification with a third-person character can be much more intense. Perhaps that's why it's traditionally been the choice for most fiction.

What about second person? Where does that put you in the story? If you're like a lot of people, "You walked to the store" triggers an immediate, "No, I didn't." That's residue from child days: second person is the voice of parents and teachers. Unless we go along willingly — choose to become a student or to read a book that's in teaching voice — the use of second person can raise hackles. If you can get around your reader's objections, however, second person can be a way to bring your reader in even closer than you can with first person. One of the best examples of the successful use of second person is Jay McInerney's *Bright Lights, Big City,* which begins like this:

IT'S SIX A.M.
DO YOU KNOW
WHERE YOU ARE?

You are not the kind of guy who would be at a place like this at this time of the morning. But here you are, and you cannot say that the terrain is entirely unfamiliar, although the details are fuzzy. You are at a nightclub talking to a girl with a shaved head. The club is either Heartbreak or the Lizard Lounge. All might come clear if you could just slip into the bathroom and do a little more Bolivian Marching Powder. Then again, it might not. A small voice inside you insists that this epidemic lack of clarity is a result of too much of that already. The night has already turned on that imperceptible pivot where two A.M. changes to six A.M. You know this moment has come and gone, but you are not yet willing to concede that you have crossed the line beyond which all is gratuitous damage and the palsy of unraveled nerve endings. Somewhere back there you could have cut your losses, but you rode past that moment on a comet trail of white powder and now you are trying to hang on to the rush. Your brain at this moment is composed of brigades of tiny Bolivian soldiers. They are tired and muddy from their long march through the night. There are holes in their boots and they are hungry. They need to be fed. They need the Bolivian Marching Powder.

A vaguely tribal flavor to this scene — pendulous jewelry, face paint, ceremonial headgear and hair styles. You feel that there is also a certain Latin theme — something more than the piranhas cruising your bloodstream and the fading buzz of marimbas in your brain.

With the choice of second person, McInerney brings the reader as close into the story as it's possible to do. (This is the interactive cinema that futurists talk about.) We're not watching this character; we are this character. And notice how McInerney does this. He creates an alter ego for the reader: "You are not the kind of guy who would be at a place like this at this time of the morning." Instead of triggering the usual "not me" reaction he would have gotten if he'd said, "Here you are; the club is either the Heartbreak or the Lizard Lounge," he lets the reader enter the story by saying, in essence, "I know *you* would never be here." It's like having diplomatic immunity. You can say, do, think, feel, be anything you want because *it's not really you.*

The second choice that affects the voice in your story is: *at what distance?* Here's where I want you to think of a camera. Put yourself behind the movie camera; you're looking through the lens at the scene. If you walk up to six inches from someone's face with the camera, what kind of a story are you telling? And if you back off until you're across the room and look through the camera, what kind of a story are you telling? That's the distance I mean.

A lot of times in the beginning of a story, there'll be what movie makers call an establishing shot: The camera first gives us the scene from far away, but then it moves in, closer and closer. A good example comes from Salvatore La Puma's "Inside the Fire":

> Where the elevated line over New Utrecht Avenue curved into the air space over 16th Avenue the three- and four-storied walk-ups on both sides were so close to the train tracks that even the arc light of this August morning couldn't reach Sergio and the others who lived on the sidewalks below. The shops there were also nearly in constant darkness with customers who came in only to look for a bargain or if shops on other streets had closed up for the day. Besides a lack of light there was also a lack of quiet on the avenue. The noise day and night of train wheels grinding by sounded like prison doors to some of the guys who now lived on the sidewalks. Some of the longtimers had become a little deaf from the train noise and those guys whenever they had something to say would shout it, even if at that moment no trains passed by to shout over. In that way too, and with his hands cupped at his mouth for a megaphone besides, Sergio Rinaldo shouted this morning to his friend, Giancarlo, that he would give Becky a party tomorrow on her fortieth birthday. She had told him and others about it over the past few weeks. While Sergio pondered where and how to get the party fixings, Giancarlo should go around to invite the others. Up and down the avenue then Giancarlo shouted the invitation to lots of homeless guys and to the few homeless women, and some shouted back that they would come to the party.
>
> "Eight guys and two dames said they'd come," said Giancarlo that night in Sergio's cellar.

Notice how the camera starts wide and high: we're up four stories at least. Then it closes a bit and focuses on the street in this particular spot under the el. Finally it closes in on Sergio and Giancarlo. If you were to read "Inside the Fire," you'd notice that the distance shifts very little throughout the story, mainly closing in to the distance in the excerpt's last line and backing off to that of the second to the last line. The range stays between the two.

I used a reverse establishing shot in "God's Will." I started with the camera exceedingly close —

> Justice arose from his bed, pushed his feet into his cracked, dusty boots with the tongue curling toward the leather laces, and, without lighting the lamp, walked in his long johns to the shelf where he kept his Bible. Holding it in his hands, he fell to his knees and thanked God for his dream.

Then I backed it off:

> Then, although it was the Sabbath, he dressed in his best suit, saddled his horse, and rode east from his one room house, over his fields, toward the flat horizon, following the pictures the Lord had laid in his mind.
>
> It was a good two hours before he came to the farm. He could hear the music from a ways off, a fiddling coming from the barn, the sound of feet stomping and laughter. He didn't take to music and would have turned around, but this too had been part of his dream. He rode to the side of the barn and tied his horse to the door handle of a Model T.

From this point on in the story, the camera stays pretty much at the distance in the last sentence. Unlike "Inside the Fire," there's no range to speak of. Even in the last scene of the story, you're seeing Justice from this far back. And that's important. Imagine if I'd kept the camera as close as it was in the first paragraph — or worse: as close as La Puma did? It would have been too hard to be that close to this kind of a person through the length of a short story. This is the discomfort to which Rita Mae Brown referred.

Obviously the power of this choice is like that of person: it lets you determine how closely your reader identifies with your main character. But it does more as well. By eliminating any range for the camera in "God's Will," I was able to create an eerie effect. (The kind of effect we might feel if we were in the presence of someone with little affect.) The only significant shift in camera is when we come close to learn of Naomi:

> They'd walk among the trees, and she'd talk. She told him about her mother who had died nearly three years before, about her brothers who were married and her sister who lived with her husband in the big city that Naomi hoped one day to see. She talked of her two younger sisters and the brother still at home, and what a handful they were, but how much she loved them, and how she wanted children, many children, just like them. And she talked of her father as though he brought light to the earth.

Because of the contrast created, bringing the camera in close on Naomi helps to later intensify the horror of the rape. It also differentiates her as a character, but works later to show how Justice subsumed her spirit.

So *at what distance* provides information about characters and their relationships; it creates atmosphere; it sets the tone in the story. It's a choice that's instrumental in giving us our story's voice.

There's another aspect of distance: "How close in time?" *Once upon a time* or *When people roamed the Wild West* or *She shopped each Saturday at the five and dime* or *Today the jam is boiling.* See how each automatically changes the voice of the story? We respond to each unconsciously, coming into the story primed with the expectation created by this distance in time.

Those then are the two aspects of *at what distance?*: camera and the specific place in time.

The third choice is *with what knowledge?* Sometimes people break this up into a whole bunch of categories that only make it more confusing than it needs to be. Your choices are really only three: omniscient, limited omniscient, and objective.

OMNISCIENT: Gives us, as the name implies, total knowledge because it's a god's eye view of the world: God sees all, hears all, knows all. Omniscient is being privy to anything and everything. We can know any character's thoughts; we can see the world in a way that a single human observer never can.

LIMITED OMNISCIENT: Lets us have access to one person's thoughts and one person's thoughts only. It's the one we're most familiar with because in our time, it's has been the most common writing choice. John Gardner traces its origins to the philosophical death of God and says that it "makes narcissists of us all." I'd say the first part of the equation is right, but that the narcissism wasn't produced by the limited omniscient, merely recorded by it.

OBJECTIVE: This, of course, is Hemingway's voice. Its use is also something people attribute to Hemingway, though there are some who argue it was around way before him. The objective voice is reportage. Some call it journalistic voice. Supposedly, in the objective voice, we enter no character's thoughts, there's no narrator in the story telling us how the events should be perceived, and, of course, there's no "author intrusion" of the sort so popular with Tolstoy. But even Hemingway had trouble holding to the objective path: As an example, in "The Snows of Kilimanjaro" he wrote:

> The cot the man lay on was in the wide shade of a mimosa tree and as he looked out past the shade onto the glare of the plain there were three of the big birds squatted obscenely, while in the sky a dozen more sailed, making quick-moving shadows as they passed.

Now for birds to squat "obscenely," we're either in this character's thoughts or there's a teller of the tale lurking around somewhere. In fact, even in the story considered the most objective of his stories — "Hills Like White Elephants" — Hemingway does take us into the character's thoughts.

Those are your three choices: Will you use first, second, or third person? At what distance in time and camera range will you tell your story? And how much information will you give your reader? Once you choose, stick to your choices. Shifting any of these in mid-story will jar your readers, bumping them out of the dream. Too big of a bump, and you risk losing your reader altogether.

So give your reader a game plan. Show right up front how the story is to be read. If you're going to be shifting in any way in the story, let your reader know early on. The reader will accept any convention you present as long as you set up the rules of the game at the beginning. Here's an example of an author doing just that. Naguib Mahfouz, who won the 1988 Nobel Prize for Literature, began *The Thief and the Dogs* in this way:

> Once more he breathed the air of freedom. But there was stifling dust in the air, almost unbearable heat, and no one was waiting for him; nothing but his blue suit and gym shoes.
>
> As the prison gate and its unconfessable miseries receded, the world — streets belabored by the sun, careening cars, crowds of people moving or still — returned.
>
> No one smiled or seemed happy. But who of these people could have suffered more than he had, with four years lost, taken from him by betrayal? And the hour was coming when he would confront them, when his rage would explode and burn, when those who had betrayed him would despair unto death, when treachery would pay for what it had done.
>
> *Nabawiyya. Ilish. Your two names merge in my mind. For years you will have been thinking about this day, never imagining, all the while, that the gates would ever actually open. You'll be watching now, but I won't fall into the trap. At the right moment, instead, I'll strike like Fate.*

We know from the very beginning how to read the book. We know that not only will we be privy to this character's thoughts, but also to his thinking; however, italics will separate one from the other. By giving us the game plan early, and by holding to it throughout, Mahfouz allows us to immerse ourselves totally in the experience of the book.

I mentioned above that these three choices interweave inextricably. That weave is referred to in literary terminology as *point of view*. In *Story and Structure*, Laurence Perrine defines point of view as "The angle of vision from which a story is told." I like to substitute the word *perspective* for point of view, however, because as the definition in my *Webster's Third* suggests, point of view refers only to the thing viewed and leaves out entirely the *effect* on the viewer: "a particular position (as in space, time, development) from which something is considered or evaluated." The word perspective, on the other hand, recalls the great breakthrough in art in the 15th Century. Through the use of technique, artists could represent reality so that the viewer experienced it as real. It's that ability to evoke the experience in the reader that writing from the inside out is all about. Like a painter who can reproduce the world through a knowledge of technique, we writers can do likewise. And like painters, it's all done with a bag of tricks — a bag of tricks that it's crucial to be aware of because it gives us remarkable power to affect our readers emotionally.

Take for example the effect Mark Twain created by the choice of the classic storyteller's voice for *Baker's Bluejay Yarn*:

> When I first begun to understand jay language correctly, there was a little incident happened here. Seven years ago, the last man in this region but me moved away. There stands his house — been empty every since; a log house, with a plank roof — just one big room, and no more; no ceiling — nothing between the rafters and the floor. Well, one Sunday morning I was sitting out here in front of my cabin, with my cat, taking the sun, and looking at the blue hills, and listening to the leaves rustling so lonely in the trees, and thinking of the home away yonder in the states, that I hadn't heard from in thirteen yeas, when a bluejay lit on that house, with an acorn in his mouth, and says, "Hello, I reckon I've struck something." When he spoke, the acorn dropped out of his mouth and rolled down the roof. He cocked his head to one side, shut one eye and put the other one to the hole, like a 'possum looking down a jug; then he glanced up with his bright eyes, gave a wink or two with his wings — which signifies gratification, you understand — and says, "It looks like a hole, it's located like a hole — blamed if I don't believe it is a hole!"

This is what Perrine calls "first person point of view" because the story is told by one of the characters. But how misleading a label! What it leaves out are variations of effect that can be evoked by "the same" point of view. We lean in toward a storyteller's voice — even if we're just reading a book. There's an atavistic root here: Our genes remember sitting around the fire ring listening to tales of the hunt. This is the voice of enchantment, the voice that we know will transport us to other realms. We give ourselves over, and that's the power of the storyteller's voice.

Now look at the first paragraph of "Action Will Be Taken" by Henrich Böll, who won the Nobel Prize in 1972. Like Twain, he uses "first person point of view," but pay attention as you read to how the voice affects you.

> Probably one of the strangest interludes in my life was the time I spent as an employee in Alfred Wunsiedel's factory. By nature I am inclined more to pensiveness and inactivity than to work, but now and again prolonged financial difficulties compel me — for pensiveness is no more profitable than inactivity — to take on a so-called job. Finding myself once again at a low ebb of this kind, I put myself in the hands of the employment office and was sent with seven other fellow-sufferers to Wunsiedel's factory, where we were to undergo an aptitude test.
>
> The exterior of the factory was enough to arouse my suspicions: the factory was built entirely of glass brick, and my aversion to well-lit buildings and well-lit rooms is as strong as my aversion to work. I became even more suspicious when we were immediately served breakfast in the well-lit, cheerful coffee shop: pretty waitresses brought us eggs, coffee and toast, orange juice was served in tastefully designed jugs, goldfish pressed their bored faces against the sides of pale-green aquariums. The waitresses were so cheerful that they appeared to be bursting with good cheer. Only a strong effort of will — so it seemed to me — restrained them from singing away all day long. They were as crammed with unsung songs as chickens with unlaid eggs.
>
> Right away I realized something that my fellow-sufferers evidently failed to realize: that this breakfast was already part of the test; so I chewed away reverently, with the full appreciation of a person who knows he is supplying his body with valuable elements. I did something which normally no power on earth can make me do: I drank orange juice on an empty stomach, left the coffee and egg untouched, as well as most of the toast, got up, and paced up and down in the coffee shop, pregnant with action.

Notice the difference? Even though they're both "first person point of view," the perspective's different. Böll's story doesn't make us lean forward at all. (In fact, it might make some readers lean back a bit.) We're kept at arm's length by this voice, which is crucial to the effect Böll's attempting to achieve. If he had brought us in close enough to sit on his lap as the storyteller's voice sometimes does, how could he achieve this wry tone and keep his reader? We would have jumped off his lap and fled.

Each of these perspectives is achieved from the inside out. If you imagine clearly in your mind's eye a ring of avid listeners around you, your voice will not be the voice in "Action Will Be Taken." And likewise if you hold in your mind's eye an image of your audience as someone at the end of the postal route, you won't write in the voice of "Baker's Bluejay Yarn." Never write for an audience; but always have an audience in your mind's eye when you're trying to find your story's voice.

Let's take a look at another perspective with the "same" point of view. Notice what Anne Beattie does in the first four paragraphs of "Jacklighting":

> It is Nicholas's birthday. Last year he was alive, and we took him presents; a spiral notebook he pulled the pages out of, unable to write but liking the sound of paper tearing; magazines he flipped through, paying no attention to pictures, liking the blur of color. He had a radio, so we could not take a radio. More than the radio, he seemed to like the sound the metal drawer in his bedside table made, sliding open, clicking shut. He would open the drawer and look at the radio. He rarely took it out.
>
> Nicholas's brother Spence has made jam. For days the cat has batted grapes around under the huge home-made kitchen table; dozens of bloody rags of cheesecloth have been thrown into the trash. There is grape jelly, raspberry jelly, strawberry, quince and lemon. Last month, a neighbor's pig escaped and ate Spence's newly planted fraise des bois plants, but overlooked the strawberry plants close to the house, heavy with berries. After that, Spence captured the pig and called his friend Andy, who came for it with his truck and took the pig to his farm in Warrenton. When Andy got home and looked in the back of the truck, he found three piglets curled against the pig.
>
> In this part of Virginia, it is a hundred degrees in August. In June and July you can smell the ground, but in August it has been baked dry; instead of smelling the earth you

smell flowers, not breeze. There is a haze over the Blue Ridge Mountains that stays in the air like cigarette smoke. It is the same color as the eye shadow Spence's girlfriend, Pammy, wears. The rest of us are sunburned, with pink mosquito bites on our bodies, small scratches from gathering raspberries. Pammy has just arrived from Washington. She is winter-pale. Since she is ten years younger than the rest of us, a few scratches wouldn't make her look as if she belonged, anyway. She is in medical school at Georgetown, and her summer-school classes have just ended. She arrived with leather sandals that squeak. She is exhausted and sleeps half the day, upstairs, with the fan blowing on her. All weekend the big fan has blown on Spence, in the kitchen, boiling and bottling his jams and jellies. The small fan blows on Pammy.

Wynn and I have come from New York. Every year we borrow his mother's car and drive from Hoboken to Virginia.

This is writing from the inside out at its best. The character tells us much about him or herself (the gender isn't ever specified) by telling us so little. You never think to it, but you unconsciously know by the end of the fourth paragraph that this character keeps a lot inside; this is one of those people for whom other people come first, possibly a self-effacing person. That's a pretty powerful effect to have on your reader — to create a dimensional character in so few words. And that comes from getting the right perspective. We don't consciously chose first person, present tense, fairly close camera, and limited omniscience. But by writing from the inside out, all of this falls into place.

There's only one way I know to get the voice right, and that's by digging a lot of clay. Sometimes it clicks early, but usually it takes days (or even weeks) for me to get all the tumblers in a row. I've found a shortcut, though: For everything I write, I do what I call *perspective trials*.

PERSPECTIVE TRIALS

Take the story on which you've been digging the clay and write it in first person with a storyteller's voice. Then write it from first person as though you're writing a letter to someone. Have it be a letter to a friend; have it be a letter to an enemy; have it be a letter to a stranger, a newspaper — it doesn't matter. Pick an audience. Just play around with this; play around with straight first person — again using the material of your story — like Ann Beattie does: real bald. Just tell your story real bald. Play around with having different narrators in your story. See what it's like if your narrator is your main character like in Böll's story, or if the person telling the story isn't the main character, but is an observer. Just try these and see what happens. Remember all the stuff about distance and where the camera is in the story. Just play around. Try second person; see what happens when you do second person with different distances in time and camera. Do third person. Especially play around with the third person omniscient *moral* voice because it's not used today; and the very fact it's not used today might make for a dynamite story because people would say, "Wow, what a unique voice." This moral voice is Dostoevsky; this moral voice is Tolstoy. It's no wonder that Mahfouz uses it because he taught himself to write fiction by reading these guys.

Here's *Midaq Alley*:

> Many things combine to show that Midaq Alley is one of the gems of times gone by and that it once shone forth like a flashing star in the history of Cairo. Which Cairo do I mean? That of the Fatimids, the Mamluks or the Sultans? Only God and the archaeologists know the answer to that, but in any case, the alley is certainly an ancient relic and precious one. How could it be otherwise with its stone-paved surface leading directly to the historic Sanadiqiyya Street? And then there is its coffee-shop known as "Kirsha's." Its walls decorated with multicolored arabesques, now crumbling, give off strong odors from the medicines of olden times, smells which have now become the spices and folk-cures of today and tomorrow . . .
>
> Although Midaq Alley lives in almost complete isolation from all surrounding activity, it clamors with a distinctive and personal life of its own. Fundamentally and basically, its roots connect with life as a whole and yet, at the same time, it retains a number of secrets of a world now past.

There's some patriarch in there telling you how not just to read the story, but how to live your life as well. You know that voice, don't you? So play with that; see what happens.

The way I want you to do these perspective trials is in quick bursts because I don't want your analytical mind to get engaged here. So whatever works for you: one minute, two minutes, five minutes; but don't go beyond five minutes. Switch back and forth; play around with them. Set a timer, and do first person for one minute; then switch to another voice / camera angle / distance in time. Try "once upon a time," and see what happens. What you're doing with these perspective trials is the tumbler routine: you're trying to get all the tumblers to fall into place. And when you do, it's so exciting because the story starts telling itself. You can't keep it from pouring out of you; it just takes off — it's just romping. And that's what you're aiming for. Until you get to THAT voice, you're just like Doctorow was before he got the voice in *Billy Bathgate:* You know the story, but you just can't write the darn thing. So this is why you try different perspectives: to get the voice. I do this with everything that I write. I go through perspective trials, usually for a couple days, because the voice doesn't come automatically. Very, very rarely do you know the voice. When you do perspective trials and the voice starts coming through — Ah! It's wonderful.

Now I want you to stop for a minute and reflect. Did you notice how my voice switched in the last three paragraphs? That's because the words starting with "Take the story on which you've been digging the clay . . . " come from a transcript of a *How to Build a Short Story* class on perspective. This is what I mean about audience affecting voice — I was talking to my students. You may not have been consciously aware of it at the time, but that shift in voice affected you. It may even have made you uncomfortable, which is what happens when the game plan's changed. This is what I mean by the power of voice. Be aware of it because it's one of your most potent fiction writing tools. And, lesson aside, the advice I give above should serve you in doing perspective trials. The key word is *play.* If you roam from perspective to perspective in these very quick bursts, one of them will resonate — eventually. And when it does, your story will just start telling itself.

Sometimes, though, we've written our story. It's done, but it just doesn't sing. That's a good indication that there's something wrong with the perspective we're telling it in. It's easy to go back and recast it. I've done that with several of my stories, but the one that gave me greatest pause was one that wanted to be written in a way I refused to consider — first person, present tense.

When it comes to writing, we all have our pet peeves, our *bêtes noires*. Mine used to be present-tense stories. And the reason I hated (not too strong a word) present tense stories is I felt puppeted by them; I felt jerked around; I felt like somebody was saying to me, "Walk into this room, stand there, no don't sit . . ." It threw me out of the story every time. I felt I couldn't participate, and that's why I read. I like that vicarious experience. Instead I was being forced into the position of a voyeur: I was in the audience, watching. Bobbie Ann Mason confessed that's why she uses present tense. This comes from a September 1, 1985 *Chicago Tribune* article by Richard Panek:

> For instance, she told the students that critics have often questioned her persistent use of the present tense, and her response has been evasive.
>
> "I always make something up, like: `It's our times,'" she said. "But," she added, "it's occurred to me that the real reason for it is the movie camera, because that's the way the camera works: Look at this, here, now."

I read that and said, "But movies are movies! They're wonderful in and of themselves. Reading is a completely different experience. Why denude it of the stuff that's beyond the stuff that movies give us? To limit it to that voyeur plane is a travesty." Rita Mae Brown agreed. In *Starting from Scratch* she wrote:

> Aside from providing the energy in a sentence, every verb is a clock. Coded into the word itself is the time of the action. So, present tense is exactly that. Unfortunately, a rash of novels in the last decade have been written in the present tense. It's a fad and it won't last. There are good reasons for writing in the past tense.
>
> The first is familiarity. Every story we've read since The Iliad has been written in past tense. Don't argue with thousands of years of success.
>
> The second reason is that the reader needs and wants

distance and protection from the story. This safety zone, provided by the past tense, allows the reader eventually to open up for the emotional impact of the story. You've got to vault your reader's defenses. The reader doesn't want to get hurt, yet you want that reader to identify with your characters and that means to feel their pain and their joy. I feel strongly about this. You have no moral right to disturb them unless you also entertain them. Art is moral passion married to entertainment. Moral passion without entertainment is propaganda, and entertainment without moral passion is television. By using the past tense (except in your dialogue, of course) you enable your reader to come to you.

I used Brown's quote like a Bible passage, sermonizing in class. Finally I *heard* myself and thought, "This is really bad; you know you have to get over this. You've got all these students who are writing — or want to write if they think they could get it by the teacher — in present tense." And so I started looking at present tense, examining its use more closely.

One of the clues to me that present tense *might* work was when I realized Truman Capote's *A Christmas Memory* — one of my all-time favorites — was first person, present tense. And that made me realize that it's all in the way you do it — and *why* you do it. Capote does it to include the reader, which was paradoxical to me until I analyzed how he did it. Here are the opening paragraphs:

Imagine a morning in late November. A coming of winter morning more than twenty years ago. Consider the kitchen of a spreading old house in a country town. A great black stove is its main feature; but there is also a big round table and a fireplace with two rocking chairs placed in front of it. Just today the fireplace commenced its seasonal roar.

A woman with shorn white hair is standing at the kitchen window. She is wearing tennis shoes and a shapeless gray sweater over a summery calico dress. She is small and sprightly, like a bantam hen; but, due to a long youthful illness, her shoulders are pitifully hunched. Her face is remarkable — not unlike Lincoln's, craggy like that, and tinted by sun and wind; but it is delicate too, finely boned, and her eyes are sherry-colored and timid. "Oh my," she exclaims, her breath smoking the windowpane, "it's fruitcake weather!

The person to whom she is speaking is myself. I am

seven; she is sixty-something. We are cousins, very distant ones, and we have lived together — well, as long as I can remember.

Look at what he does here. There's no puppeting going on. He's so genteel in the way he asks our permission to do what he's doing. He says, "Imagine." Even though that's the imperative, he doesn't jerk you. "Imagine a morning in late November." You can say "No, I don't want to" and put the book aside. But he invites you in — if you want to come.

And then look what he does with distance in time. First we have: "A coming of winter morning more than twenty years ago." He moves us into time and place. It isn't just the words "twenty years ago" that take us back; it's the rhythm of that whole sentence. It's as powerful in it's ability to transport as "Once upon a time." We lean forward into the story.

Then another imperative: "Consider." It resonates with the first imperative, and we find ourselves imagining what the camera now shows us: the well-chosen details that bring us fully into the dream. And he makes sure he's got the reader in the dream before he shifts the *distance in time* to present tense: "Just today the fireplace commenced its seasonal roar." By this point, the reader isn't an observer, but a participant. He's allowed us to tag along if we want.

And then we see the woman: not as somebody up there on a big screen, but right there in the room with us. We are present in the story even though the story's in present tense. And by the time we realize it's a present-tense story, we're too firmly in the scene to be excluded. We're along for the ride!

Capote convinced me that it was all in how you did it. And he showed me present tense had its use. It wasn't essential to throw the baby out with the bath water. I finally succumbed and let my story tell itself from the perspective it wanted to be told. The result surprised me. First person, present tense gave me the ability to let the reader enter not just the main character's thoughts, but his *thought process.* And that was all it took to change a story that had seemed too much a "woman as victim" story to a story about the abuse of power. Capote's lesson stood me in good stead: it's all in how you use it.

One of the most powerful uses of present tense can be found in David Morrell's "The Beautiful Uncut Hair of Graves," which won the Horror Writers of America novella award in 1991. The story begins,

> Despite the rain, you've been to the cemetery yet again, ignoring the cold autumn gusts slanting under your bowed umbrella, the drenched drab leaves blowing against your soaked pant legs and shoes.
>
> Two graves. You shiver, blinking through tears toward the freshly laid sod. There aren't any tombstones. There won't be for a year. But you imagine what the markers look like, each birth date different, the death dates—God help you—the same.

As you can see, the story is in the second person — a risky choice as it is because second person tends to distance the reader. Here, however, we see a real master at work. Morrell creates the scene with sensory detail so that the reader is drawn into the body of the character, feeling the cold, the rain along with him. Once he has us there, Morrell starts the present-tense movie. We're trapped behind the screen. Through the power of sensory detail, he's made us participants in his movie.

That's what perspective's about: it's a powerful tool that unlocks the voice of our story and concomitantly brings our readers along for the ride.

CHAPTER SEVEN

How To Birth A Story

Up to this point, you've been digging the clay. It's all been preparation. Think of it like pregnancy: you've conceived and the fertilized egg has gone through differentiation and now you're just gestating. Now's the time to partner with your unconscious and to let it do the work for you.

Doing nothing. This is often the hardest part of the writing process. An essential part of the creative process is to do just that — nothing. During this period, we allow; we trust the process; we let the unconscious do its work. And, paradoxically, without any conscious effort on our part, our creative product will grow inside of us until its ready to be born.

Like most writers, Bertrand Russell knew the power of incubation. When working on a book, he'd do all the research, and then he metaphorically put the book on the shelf. When it was time to sit down and write the book, he knew it; the words flowed out of him without any conscious effort on his part. He said it was as though he were a scribe. He only had to let his pen take its course. It must have worked: He won the Nobel Prize for Literature in 1950.

The English philosopher Herbert Spencer, who coined the phrase "survival of the fittest," talked of the power of incubation in his autobiography. He reported a conversation with George Eliot (Mary Ann Evans) where "she said that, considering how much thinking I must have done, she was surprised to see no lines on my forehead." He told her that was because he was never puzzled, to which she responded: "O! that's the most arrogant thing I ever heard uttered."

No, said Spencer, not if she understood his meaning: " And I then proceeded to explain that my mode of thinking did not involve that concentrated effort which is commonly accompanied by wrinkling of the brow." He went on to describe his way of problem solving — a method akin to Russell's, but Spencer tended to stir the pot from time to time when a new observation would trigger an association.

> And thus, little by little, in unobtrusive ways, without conscious intention or appreciable effort, there would grow up a coherent and organized theory. Habitually the process was one of slow unforced development, often extending over years; and it was, I believe, because the thinking done went on in this gradual, almost spontaneous way, without strain, that there was an absence of those lines of thought which Miss Evans remarked — an absence almost as complete thirty years later, notwithstanding the amount of thinking done in the interval.
>
> I name her remark, and give this explanation, partly to introduce the opinion that a solution reached in the way described is more likely to be true than one reached in pursuance of a determined effort to find a solution. The determined effort causes perversion of thought. When endeavoring to recollect some name or thing which has been forgotten, it frequently happens that the name or thing sought will not arise in consciousness; but when attention is relaxed, the missing name or thing often suggest itself. While thought continues to be forced down certain wrong turnings which had originally been taken, the search is in vain; but with the cessation of strain the true association of ideas has an opportunity of asserting itself. And, similarly, it may be that while an effort to arrive forthwith at some answer to a problem, acts as a distorting factor in consciousness and causes error, a quiet contemplation of the problem from time to time, allows those proclivities of thought which have probably been caused unawares by experiences, to make themselves felt, and to guide the mind to the right conclusion.

So it is with writing. It isn't remarkable that after twelve years incubation "Flowering Judas" sprang full-blown from Katherine Anne Porter's pen "between seven o'clock and midnight of a very cold December, 1929, in Brooklyn." It's only remarkable that Porter left a record of the process — a process that's so common most writers don't even note it. Stories often birth themselves in just this way, stewing in our unconscious for days or months or years and then arriving in an unignorable rush that's as insistent as any child wanting to be born.

The trick is to do nothing long enough for the work to come to fruition within your unconscious — to give your storymaker time to assemble it — and that takes proof and practice. After a time, you'll believe that there's a baby growing inside — even without ultrasound to see what's going on. But because this is hard in the beginning, what follows are a couple primers for the Occidental: *What to do when you're doing nothing* and *How to do nothing with great effectiveness so that it leads to a simple and painless birth.*

So, to the first: *What to do when you're doing nothing:*

It's always important to know where we're going if we have any hope of reaching our goal. Here the goal is a finished story that pops like Athena from Zeus' head, and the only way to achieve it is through doing things that unclutter the unconscious sufficiently that it can devote full-time to the job.

This is the time to cook, build a model, swim, play chess, hike, paint, play music, or repair a toaster — whatever it is that puts you into that "time out of time state" where you lose all track of time. What you're looking for are activities that allow you to *immerse* yourself in the experience without thought. Every writer has them: Ernest Hemingway hunted; May Sarton gardened; D. H. Lawrence made love. Whatever takes you away from the ceaseless round of chatter unclutters the unconscious. Look at what works for you and make it a point of including it in your day — not just when you're in the incubation phase, but every day because you'll discover that each day takes you through the same cycle of creativity in an abbreviated way. Each day that you write, you conceive and differentiate and gestate and birth; and each day, you'll need to replenish the well through some wordless activities.

For me, painting is the best immersion activity I've ever found. I can so lose myself in the process that I forget to eat. When I stop, I discover hours have passed and think, "Where did the time go?" While I'm painting, I'm not thinking. But more important, I'm not floating vague in a sea of no-thought: I'm doing what Aldous Huxley thought so important he had birds in his fictional country in *Island* crying, "Attention, attention, attention." I am focused in on what I'm doing with a concentrated effort of attention.

There's an added benefit to this sort of immersion. Mihaly Csikszentmihalyi in *Beyond Boredom and Anxiety* referred to "the holistic sensation that people feel when they act with total involvement" by the name it has been given across cultures and throughout centuries: *flow*. In his book *Flow: The Psychology of Optimal Experience*, he showed how to use flow to bring happiness to our lives. But that's something artists have always known: There's no more feared state than when the well's run dry. The sheer act of creating brings joy. And as Pierre Teilhard de Chardin said, "Joy is the most infallible sign of the presence of God."

Csikszentmihalyi discovered twenty-five years ago that people who immersed themselves in activities that challenged them enough, but not too much, experienced a satisfaction in their lives that those who did not never felt. He studied chess players and rock climbers and brain surgeons, and he found that no matter the occupation, the immersion coupled with the appropriate challenge put the person into the flow state. Having been a rock climber myself, I knew what he was talking about. When I'd be moving up a rock face, time would stand still. Everything would become vivid: details would stand out with a clarity that seemed almost drug-induced. Light hitting my drop of sweat on the rock would turn it into a jewel; strands of fur on a spider's back would be so discrete it was as though I saw them through a magnifying glass. But most heavenly was the loss of the "me" in the activity. It's that *loss of self* that gives the bliss to immersion activities.

So there's one answer to *What to do when you're doing nothing* writing-wise: Do anything that allows you to immerse yourself fully in the activity and at the same time challenges you enough, but not too much. Not meditation, not relaxation — concentration, attention. Do anything that is but write. During this stage of the process don't let yourself write one word. And, similarly, don't let yourself talk your story to anyone. Now more than ever, talking it will dissipate the energy. Keeping your story inside with no outlet creates a pressure-cooker sensation — eventually you feel as though you're going to explode if you can't let your story out. And that's the sensation you're aiming for. The silence of immersion activities helps build that pressure.

What about the second primer: *How to do nothing with great effectiveness so that it leads to a simple and painless birth*? For fWesterners, this is the most fun because it isn't so *hands off* as immersion. We can really feel we're doing something to partner our unconscious — even though we *are* letting go and trusting the unconscious to do the work for us. I call this *active incubation* because we're building bridges between the conscious and the unconscious mind.

One of these bridges you probably know well: How often have you said, "Let me sleep on it"? It's one of the best problem-solving tools we've got. And it works for writing, too. In fact, so well that I've come to the conclusion that I couldn't write a darn thing worth publishing if I couldn't sleep on it. I recently had an experience with that. I'd been asked by an editor to add 1,000 words to an article on Continuum Trait, my theory discussed in Chapter Five. I did it, but it wasn't first-rate and, worse, the voice was off — it didn't match that of the first part of the article. Still, it seemed as good as I was going to be able to do.

I went to bed that night, intending to touch it up in the morning and send it. But the next morning I got up and completely changed the whole thing — not from my conscious mind, but like Russell, as though I were transcribing. The words came that easily. Not only was there a logical flow that hadn't been there the day before, but the voice matched.

That's the power of sleeping on it. I've come to trust the process, and like Dr. Jonas Salk, to depend on it. In an article in *Administration Management* he said, "It is always with excitement that I wake up in the morning wondering what my intuition will toss up to me, like gifts from the sea. I work with it, and rely upon it. It's my partner."

From sleeping on it, we wake with *knowings* that seem to come out of nowhere or we wake from dreams that show us what it is we need to know. The latter I illustrated in my article, "The Creative Personality," which first appeared in 1985 in Piedmont Airlines' magazine.

An example of creativity is shown in the story of the German chemist Friedrich August Kekulé von Stradonitz, who is commonly referred to as, simply, Kekulé. He had been working for some time on determining the structure of the benzene molecule. He was having little success until he dreamed one night of six snakes forming a circle by each biting the tail of the snake in front of it. Upon awakening, Kekulé remembered his dream image, and he recognized that this image might be symbolizing the structure of the benzene molecule. As it turns out, benzene is a hexagonal ring structure with six carbon atoms arranged at the vertexes. It was Kekulé's dream that led him to his discovery.

I hope you've noticed a common thread in these anecdotes. None of these breakthroughs was serendipitous. Kekulé's eureka came as the result of the studying and researching and hypothesizing and testing that he'd done *before* he had this dream. My ease with writing the 1,000 words came only after I'd put in the time writing the day before. That's what creativity's about: giving the unconscious enough to work with so that the breakthroughs can come — like they did for Dr. Salk:

After tedious, long-drawn-out experiments seeking ways to immunize against polio, Salk made one morning, upon awakening, an intuitive leap to the correct vaccine.

That's what you've been doing (though I hope it's not "tedious" — a word choice that tells more about the author of the article than Salk). By digging all the clay you've been digging through the last chapters, you've given your unconscious the material with which to work.

We can build the bridges during sleep, and we can build them during our waking hours. Do you need to fast? I've never done it, so I can't say. But there's a clue here: Without food, we wouldn't have the energy to think in an analytical way — one of the most calorie-burning things our body does. And it's when the analytical thoughts finally stop that the breakthroughs most often come. In *The Creative Process* edited by Brewster Ghiselin, the famous mathematician Henri Poincaré recounted a breakthrough of his own:

Just at this time I left Caen, where I was then living, to go on a geologic excursion under the auspices of the school of mines. The changes of travel made me forget my mathematical work. Having reached Coutances, we entered an omnibus to go some place or other. At the moment, when I put my foot on the step the idea came to me, without anything in my former thoughts seeming to have paved the way for it, that the transformations I had used to define the Fuchsian functions were identical with those of non-Euclidean geometry. I did not verify the idea; I should not have had time, as, upon taking my seat in the omnibus, I went on with a conversation already commenced, but I felt a perfect certainty. On my return to Caen, for conscience's sake I verified the result at my leisure.

Poincaré's breakthrough came because in that moment he wasn't trying for a breakthrough. He had *gotten out of his own way,* and with his analytical mind silenced, he could hear his unconscious speak. The literature on creativity is ripe with such accounts. You can probably think of a few such experiences yourself. Names we couldn't remember an hour before come as soon as we get into the mind-numbing rhythm of vacuuming. In the middle of the night we wake knowing what it is we forgot to buy at the store. It's by turning off the analytical process that we build the bridge between the unconscious and the conscious mind.

I make use of active incubation every day I write. I don't take a shower *until* I get stuck in my writing for the day because invariably a shower will be where ideas pop up. In my journal entry for March 25, 1990, I recorded the birth of my book *Dream Warriors* and its main character. Here's a part of the entry:

> Shower thoughts: Daphne, I thought; I'll call her Daphne . . . Oh, another shower thought: I heard Daphne say, "I see a man. A shadow, big, burly like a rugby player. He's wearing a sweater, I think. Or a shirt. Oh, what do you Americans call them? Perspiration shirt?"

The book actually sprang into my conscious mind while I was in the shower. And that's not an isolated incident: My writing logs and journals are filled with "shower thought" notations.

Other things that shift me from that "stuck" tip-of-the-iceberg place include water as well: I love to sit by a waterfall or any running water — even the fountains in shopping malls will do. It's the negative ions, I've heard. Running, splashing water produces negative ions, which are supposed to relax people. That's why planners put fountains in malls: Relaxed people stay longer and buy more. The stir of water, the mist. That's, also, what lets the storymaker speak. Running water's my way of actively incubating.

Find your own. Some writers get unstuck sitting by a fire; others with candlelight — two more sources of negative ions. Some writers use still water — lakes to float in, hot tubs to sink into. In fact, I've heard of writers who do all their writing in the bathtub. Other writers couldn't write if they couldn't drive. One of my students puts Grieg on the car stereo and drives across the desert, preferably during lightning storms. I drive in silence with a pad of paper at hand to scribble down the *knowings* that surface from the well. Some people meditate — sitting meditation or walking meditation; it doesn't matter. Anything that stops analytical thought lets the knowings surface. And when they do, you'll say with Poincaré, "I felt a perfect certainty." That's what it's like when the unconscious speaks: *You know that you know, even though you don't know how it is that you know.* A perfect certainty! And just a suggestion: always keep a small notebook with you all the time when you're incubating. We forget our breakthroughs — momentous as they seem. Write them down!

So part of the answer to *How to do nothing with great effectiveness so that it leads to a simple and painless birth* is merely to get out of our own way and let the knowings come.

Active Incubation

There's more, though, to active incubation than just getting out of your own way. This is the time to actively partner your unconscious as well. One way to do that is through your nightly recap. Instead of using the time to recall your day, use it to focus on your story. Each night during the gestation period, lie in bed in the dark and see your story as clearly as you can; let all the details come alive for you. Summon the smells, tastes, textures, emotions, sounds. Make it as vivid as you can. And each night after you've fleshed your story out like this, say to your storymaker, "What I'd really like is some help on this story. I know you're really good at this, so I'll just turn it over to you, and while I sleep, finish this for me, will you?" And it helps to give your storymaker a time frame; our unconscious works best with a schedule. So every night add something like this: "By the end of the week, we're going to have to birth this baby. We've got three days!"

The next night, do another, fuller recap, and make the same request of the storymaker. Do this each night until the due date. You may find yourself in a state like Robert Louis Stevenson, who "was thrashing about in his bed one night, greatly alarming his wife. She woke him up, infuriating Stevenson, who yelled, `I was dreaming a fine bogey tale!' The nightmare from which he had been unwillingly extracted was the premise for the story *Dr. Jekyll and Mr. Hyde.*"

When you wake in the morning after doing such nightly recaps, follow up in this way: Don't get out of bed. Stay where you are, making only enough movement to pick up your already open notebook and already uncapped pen. Write without thinking — anything about your story that comes to mind. Write for at least five minutes *before* you get out of bed. Then close your notebook *without* reading what you've written. You'll be reading it later — when gestation comes to an end. To read it too soon flips you into analytical thought. This is your storymaker's turn, not your critic's. That comes after the story is birthed — when we get to do what we never get to do with our kids: revise!

Using your nightly recap to actively incubate is one way to push your story's birth. *Silent movies* is another technique that helps build the pressure to the bursting point.

                    SILENT MOVIES

Set a timer for ten minutes, and then sit without thought until it rings. If thoughts do come, don't worry about it. Just let them move through your mind without holding on to them. Be still.

Then for the next ten minutes, see your story as a movie in your mind. Make it as vivid as you can; flesh out the details as you would with a nightly recap. Go back and forth, back and forth. Stop the projector, reverse the film, run it forward again. See it more and more clearly each time it reels by. Watch, but do not let yourself write — no matter how strong the urge.

Finally, for the last ten minutes, go back to sitting quietly without any thoughts. Stay still like that until you have such a strong urge to write that you just can't resist it. Then, and only then, pick up your pen and write.

Do silent movies as often as you can during the days of your incubation period. If you can't spend a full thirty minutes on it, cut it back to five-minute segments. Even one-minute rounds can build the pressure. Remember, though: Don't read anything you write.

So that's *How to do nothing with great effectiveness so that it leads to a simple and painless birth.*

There's another aspect to incubation that's given short shrift: Artists need large amounts of solitude to create. Virginia Woolf said it plainly: a room of one's own with a lock on the door. May Sarton began *Journal of a Solitude* with a comment that she was

> here alone for the first time in weeks, to take up my `real' life again at last. That is what is strange — that friends, even passionate love, are not my real life unless there is time alone in which to explore and to discover what is happening or has happened. Without the interruptions, nourishing and maddening, this life would become arid. Yet I taste it fully only when I am alone here and the house and I resume old conversations.

Add to that what Dorothea Brande said in *Becoming a Writer*:

> The necessity which the artist feels to indulge himself in solitude, in rambling leisure, in long speechless periods, is behind most of the charges of eccentricity and boorishness that are leveled at men of genius. If the period is recognized and allowed for, it need not have a disruptive effect. The artist will always be marked by occasional periods of detachment.

If you have any doubt about the power of and necessity for time alone in your creative round, read Anthony Storr's *Solitude: A Return to the Self*, in which he explores the link between artistic genius and solitude. He says,

> But, as one would expect, imaginative capacity tends to become highly developed in gifted individuals who, for one reason or another, have passed rather solitary childhoods.

And I know from experience that solitude can be found within the crush of a large extended family. But then maybe that's because my mother believed firmly in a room of one's own with a required knock on the door. And there was always the woods.

If you didn't have solitude as a kid, it's not too late. Give yourself time alone each day even if it's only a solitary walk. Just remember to leave the portable radio at home, for as Storr says,

> The current popularity of techniques like `transcendental meditation' may represent an attempt to counterbalance the absence of silence and solitude which the modern urban environment inflicts on us.

A quiet and solitary walk can help your writing more than you'll ever know.

What if you do all this and still no birth seems imminent? You've dug the clay for weeks, and then you've immersed yourself in flow experiences; you've actively incubated with nightly recaps and silent movies; you've given yourself solitude. And nothing. What then?

BUTT TO SEAT

Here's the next step — a technique that named itself through my journal writing. On January 25, 1989 I wrote:

> I had a tough time sitting down to it again this morning, but I made myself do it, and, as usual, what came was entirely unexpected, amazing, and wowingly wonderful. Proof once

again that the muse doesn't strike; it's cajoled by dint of butt to seat.

Butt to seat. It's the best writer's technique of all. Joseph Conrad believed in it so fervently that he'd have his wife tie him to his chair and not let him up until he had written. In his autobiography, *Education of a Wandering Man*, Louis L'Amour said,

> There are so many wonderful stories to be written, and so much material to be used. When I hear people talking of writer's block, I am amazed.
>
> Start writing, no matter about what. The water does not flow until the faucet is turned on. You can sit and look at a page for a long time and nothing will happen. Start writing and it will.

That's every writer's secret: not waiting for the muse to strike. Give yourself at most a week to incubate, but when the due date arrives, sit down to write. Seldom is there a magic moment of parturition without applying butt-to-seat technique.

Beyond that, set yourself a schedule and give yourself a goal. When I was writing fiction full-time, I did it just like a job: my hours were 7:00 A.M. until noon. That was my schedule. My goal was to write five pages per day. Sometimes I finished the five pages before noon, and then I was free to stop. Sometimes I finished the five pages by noon, but if I didn't, I still stopped. It was a goal, not a stick. If you reinforce yourself for your successes and ignore your failures, you'll write much faster.

A note here: When your writing's coming easily, it's often hard to stop; it feels too good. I rarely stop if I have my five pages done before noon, for instance. But I always remembered advice that came by way of a *Paris Review* interview with Ernest Hemingway. Although like many writers, he only wrote during the morning, he said he would make a point of stopping before he'd written everything that was in him that day to write. It's great advice. If you know that the plane arrives in the next scene, it'll prime your pump the following day. If you empty the well, though, you may find as every writer has that it sometimes takes days to refill. Careful! You're still partnering with your unconscious even when the story seems to be writing itself.

Become aware of your own patterns. Although most fiction authors write only four to five hours a day, you may work best doing sixteen-hour stints for three weeks straight. Or you may find you can only write one hour a day without exhausting yourself. So schedule an hour and set a goal of a page a day. Even if you only write five days a week, you'll still have produced 260 pages in one year's time. That's a whole book! The important thing is to find your own pattern — and then make it a habit. Good habits are just as hard to break as bad ones.

And don't forget what Rollo May said in *The Courage to Create*: For the creative person, fear never goes away. How can it? When we're working with the unconscious as we must do in writing fiction, every day we walk up to the abyss and jump in. Or as a student of mine, Richard Goldstein, said, "No, you've got that wrong. You don't just walk up to the abyss and jump in. You walk up to the abyss and turn around and jump in backwards!"

A very scary process! So give yourself permission to sharpen pencils or stare out the window for ten minutes or so before you start. But don't let stage fright stop you. After your ten minutes is up, metaphorically tie yourself to your chair and stay there until your allotted hours are up whether you've written anything or not. You'll find that the sheer boredom of sitting often catalyzes a remarkable gush of words.

Once the writing's coming, though, I'm not a proponent of staying put. I graze constantly while I write, getting up every fifteen minutes or so to peel a carrot or to make some rice. My brain gets fuel, and I get to get away from the computer for a bit — essential for the eyes. Also, I keep myself from shifting too quickly into tip of the iceberg thinking if I'm always getting up: I go into mini-incubation when I'm pouring frozen peas into a bowl. By the time I'm back at the computer, a mini-eureka may have erupted.

During the birthing stage of writing, you'll be slapping your clay on the armature just as fast as you can. That involves watching the movies in the mind and chronicling; it also involves remembering that three weeks before you wrote a great scene in your clay-digging notebook, which means you have to stop and find it (and that always takes time) and then add it to the story. You just keep going day by day, until you've got the story done. By done I don't mean finished in the sense of ready for publication; I do mean done in the sense of your knowing the whole story, the shape of it — beginning, middle, and, especially, end — so that when you finally do read it to others, it can't possibly become a "written by committee" story. It's your story from start to finish; it grew out of you because you wrote it from the inside out.

CHAPTER EIGHT

THERE'S ALWAYS A CRITIC

As a writer, death and taxes aren't the only things you can count on in life. There's another: *There's always a critic.* If it isn't your own inner critic, it's someone else. And that's worse because at least we can train our inner critic. The outside critics often come like analytical desperadoes, big guns blazing, attacking anything that crosses their paths. Because fiction's an art and not a science, it leaves us particularly vulnerable to all the critics of the world — and they're everywhere: in writers groups, classes, critiques, rejections. That's why it's essential to know how to survive the critics if you're going to keep writing. The best defense is knowing *the art of critique.*

I have three rules of critique. My first is this: I *NEVER* say anything about someone's story unless I myself could fix it. Too many people give advice; very few would know how to follow their own advice. But, boy, we're game to listen to people who couldn't do it themselves. It never ceases to amaze me how perfectly intelligent people who would never consult amateurs on matters of their mental or physical or financial health will readily accept advice from their friends when it comes to critiquing their stories. Why? And worse, they'll pay attention to the comments of people who don't know what *can* be done with a story because they haven't read broadly enough to see what *has* been done through fiction's history. The best way to become your own best critic is to read, read, read. And don't just read contemporary stuff; read the stuff that's lasted. It'll give you more clues as to what stories can do.

Once you know what stories can do, you also have a pretty good idea of what you don't like. My second rule of critique is to 'fess up. We all have our *bêtes noires.* As you saw, mine used to be *present tense*: it would instantly trigger a negative reaction in me. As good critiquers, we have to understand that we have things that make us see red. I came to see how I automatically dismissed any present-tense story — and seeing it enabled me to say to myself, "Hey, watch out: it's present tense. Be objective!" Knowing what rubs us the wrong way (or the right way, for that matter) enables us to be dispassionate in our critique.

My third rule is an extension of the second: to become good at the art of critique, we must come to understand the way we all confuse "like" with "good" and "dislike" with "bad." It's perfectly legitimate to like or dislike a story. In fact, in every group, you're likely to get a bell curve on any story — that of an amateur or that of a professional, it doesn't matter. Some people will love a story; some will hate a story; and most will be somewhere in between.

In their preface to *The Minerva Book of Short Stories 1*, editors Giles Gordon and David Hughes wrote of this problem:

> The best? Despite our justification for the superlative in our introduction to a previous volume, this word still seems to irritate critics: what are our criteria of selection? In a review of our 1987 gathering, we were gently chided for playing our editorial cards too close to our chest. But surely the definition of best is simple enough, because so entirely subjective. It is what we as readers liked most without having to know why, what we most wanted to share with others, what seemed to us to add more to the savour and relevance of life than countless other very good stories did.

But when it comes to critiquing yours or another's story, just because you love it doesn't mean it's necessarily good. Besides if you said it was a "good" story because you love it, it wouldn't give much help for turning it into the most beautiful story it can possibly be.

What would?

There are two things that a good critiquer focuses on in a story, and they grow out of what a story's supposed to do and be. First of all, as *Esquire*'s longtime fiction editor Rust Hills said in his introduction to *Writing in General and the Short Story in Particular*, "a short story tells of something that happened to somebody." And, says

Hills, in a short story you have unity of effect. Two things.

So as a critiquer, you ask: "Does something happen to somebody?" And you ask: "Was there any point where I fell out of the dream" because we fall out of the dream when unity of effect is violated.

Let's start with the second question. To discover if there's any place you fall out of the dream, read your story **aloud.** You'll *hear* the places where you bump much better than you can ever *see* them. And if you find yourself losing interest, it's a sign! To me, the definition of a good story is one — my own or another's — that can be read over and over and over again without my losing interest. Reading aloud puts a story to even more of a test because it makes the analytical process subordinate to that atavistic part of us that knows a good story when it hears one. When I'm writing fiction, I sometimes form a two-person critique "group" with one other person who's good at hearing stories read aloud. The feedback of a *trained* listener can be invaluable for removing the bumps that would throw your reader out of the dream.

Now back to the first question: When Hills asks if something happens to someone, it's another way of asking "Is someone different at the end of the story than he or she was at the beginning?" If this isn't the case, it's proof that the story isn't growing out of your character's dilemma and Continuum Trait. Without a main character firmly ensconced in the middle of some very large horns, there really is no story. It's just a vignette, an anecdote. No one changes; nothing happens to anyone.

And those two things combined with my three rules are what make up the art of critique. Beyond that, the best advice I can give you is avoid untrained critics and be on the lookout for a special breed of these: *the resident critic.* To put it simply, the resident critic is the one who gets his or her needs met by the scholarly play of the analytical mind. Now, don't get me wrong; I love the scholarly play of the analytical mind. It's just that it is absolutely no good at helping us revise our stories *unless* it's been trained in the art of critique. I've worked hard to train my own analytical mind over the years. It's no easy matter. Here's an example: I mentioned I'd studied with Miriam Sagan and that in her classes we didn't critique, but merely commented on what was "hot." Invariably, what people thought was hot in my own writing were the very things I would have crossed out if we'd been allowed to cross anything out. "Wow! Imagine that," my analytical mind would say in wonder. I started paying attention. It happened almost every time. So for a while, my analytical mind translated it into this: "I think it's garbage, so it must be good." After awhile, though, it started to see the worth in these unexcised bits. And the why of the worth: they were images that had such deep taproots they were almost archetypal. But how could my analytical mind have known this? It had been trained in Socratic Method for goodness sake!

In most situations where you find resident critics, the emphasis isn't on making the analytical mind the storymaker's partner. It's more like this: Imagine a writers group where you've got a resident critic who fancies herself a playwright, though the only things she's read to the group are some unfinished one-act plays each of which she wrote in one sitting several years before. She's not writing anything at the present time. You're writing a novel that's as experiential as Durrell's *Justine*, and to do it, you've been writing on large index cards because you want to be able to shuffle them to achieve the simultaneity of experience that for you is human consciousness. The resident critic listens to you read, shifting more and more in her chair with each card. When you finish, she's the first off the block: "But where's the through line?" she asks, her brow knitted in consternation.

"Through line?" you ask.

"You know," she says in a tone that says you couldn't possibly know. "The *action line*."

"I'm not writing a play," you say, explaining once again your modus operandi.

"But you still need an action line!"

The problem with resident critics isn't the fact that they usually don't have a clue what they're talking about, it's that they talk as though they do — and with such persuasive power that everyone else in the group takes off running after the leader of the pack. The group now spends your twenty minutes talking about your absence of action line. And if you're relatively new at the game, what do you know? You'll go home and try to insert an action line. Or you'll shelve it, saying, "I'm not really much of a writer."

Resident critics don't just haunt writers groups. University writing programs also seem to attract those who wield the tongue. At one college where I taught, I used to stand in the hallway listening to a well-known fiction writer excoriating his creative writing students with comments such as this: "You're Anglos. How could you write? You have nothing to draw from. Of course your fiction is trite."

Critiquers of the resident critic ilk also suffer from the same sort of syllogistic thinking. Trapped in what Carl Becker calls the "climate of opinion," they can't see any truth but the one current. I wrote this in my journal after receiving a resident critic's critique of *Perchance to Dream*:

> As is all the rage these days, he's changed all my present participles to past tense (e.g., instead of "The coyotes were climbing through the window" he wanted "The coyotes climbed"). I think this removes a level of active meaning. Why are people so bandwagonish? I refuse to join this one. Present participles don't "stop action" any more than any other verb! (Less if you understand grammar!) "Were climbing" does two things for me: it conveys the awkwardness of the action (which should tickle the funny bone — but [the critiquer] isn't an imager) and it makes it an action in the "movies in the mind" sense I want this to be. "Climbed" can do that — sure. But it is action accomplished. Why this limit? Always some fad! I wish this one would give up the ghost.

On that note, do you know why it's "wrong" to split infinitives? Because the first grammar book was a translation of Latin rules, and in Latin it does create havoc when you split infinitives. But how awkward to write "to go boldly" or "boldly to go" when "to boldly go" tells it all! Some rules are made to be broken, but that's one you break at the peril of sounding uneducated. Too bad.

And resident critics who masquerade as editors! As my mother said once when an editor was making a mishmash of my work, "If she could write, she wouldn't be an editor." Having been on both sides of the fence, I know that isn't true — some of us just love language enough to want to make other people's words sing, too. But I have seen some resident critics among the ranks of editors. In one rejection of my story "On Top," an editor who liked it wrote: "In this story, I am particularly impressed by how the point of view draws [Bruce] into a hole; his own point of view shows how despicable he is and adds a dimension of self-awareness that makes the narration quite compelling." However, this editor failed to get another editor's second because that editor "found herself unable to feel compassion for either character." The first editor added, "Once she pointed that out, I agreed that more compassion for the characters was needed."

The power of the resident critic to sway! But what does the second editor mean by "compassion"? It's defined as "sympathetic feeling : PITY, MERCY." For Aristotle, pity came when the audience recognized the character's plight — how he, like any of them, was trapped in his own fate. What traps us more in our own fate than our psychological makeup? How could my character ever get what he wants — to know from the depths of his being that he's loved — when, as he is in this story, he's trapped in playing king of the mountain? How sad to be so locked within the cage of ourselves, playing out our own inevitable destiny.

I don't think "sympathetic feeling" is what this editor meant, though. My guess is she was saying, "I don't like these characters." That's legitimate, but it isn't a requirement of fiction. Who likes the Marquis de Sade? But these days you can't go to a writers group without someone saying he found nothing in the character to like. Yet literature's teeming with despicable characters whom we've never been asked to like before this "climate of opinion" took hold.

My theory is we want to like characters because liking them makes us feel safe in an increasingly unsafe world. But there's a lesson to be learned from the writer Ann Rule. She used to staff a rape crisis line with *Ted Bundy*. After their shift, he would walk her to her car to protect her! They became friends. She said he was a very nice man. That's how these guys work; they're manipulators: They know that being nice gets them what they want, so they're nice. In "On Top," the other character, Sarah, wouldn't be entrusting her life to Bruce if she didn't feel he was basically a likable sort of guy. My job as an author was to show her mistake in a way the reader could experience, too.

This all reminds me of an article on Joseph Wambaugh that I read a few years back in *The Los Angeles Times* magazine. Wambaugh's time on a California police force gave him the material for his crime books like *The Onion Field*. In the article, he was expressing his annoyance with reporters covering the trials of heinous killers. He said the reporters invariably wrote that the defendants showed no remorse. Of course they show no remorse, said Wambaugh. *They don't have it in them to show remorse.* That's what makes these people different from all the rest of us who would never do such things.

It's a hard lesson to learn. We've departed from the *Zeitgeist* thinking of Dostoevsky's age. Then all knew some men were just plain evil. Psychology eclipsed all that; evil died along with God. Everything can be fixed in a scientific age. We started noticing a problem, though. All this emphasis on fixing the mind hasn't eradicated the sort of people Wambaugh writes about. In fact, their ranks have grown. So as a culture that feels itself sinking, we reach for a new amulet. Unfortunately, the one we seem to have grabbed is rather solipsistic: a notion that bad things only happen because people "draw events to themselves" through their thoughts. If, they reason, they hold only good in mind, nothing bad will happen. It's a reversion to "child thought." Children think they create their world with their thoughts; they think they can make bad men go away just by believing they're not there. Con men love it! As P.T. Barnum said, there's a sucker born every minute.

No, it isn't essential to like characters, for that would take away fiction's power to wake us from our *Zeitgeist* sleep. Compassion's another story. Compassion, said the Buddha, is the vice of the sage. Wise men know the failings of all of us mere mortals — and love us anyway.

Now none of this is to say criticism isn't valuable. After your story is written, it's essential to "test drive" your work on an audience — if for no other reason than to read it aloud to another. Just pick your critics carefully. Make sure they're trained. Make sure they know the difference between "*I* don't like it" and "it's bad." One way to clue yourself in to the fact that you're dealing with a resident critic is to notice if they zero in on one thing and one thing only — action line, Anglos, present participle, compassion — and keep circling around that point. That's how the analytical mind works: It's reductionistic. Steer clear of these resident critics: it's my experience that they're untrainable. Those who aren't resident critics, though, can make very good critics indeed.

To help yourself find the critics that can actually help you write better, it's important to know what it is you're trying to achieve with your writing. If your goal is to win a Nobel Prize you need a whole different set of criteria than if you want to become *the* writer *Cosmopolitan* most likes to serialize. You've got to decide how you want to write and then stick with it even in the face of odds. To do that, it helps to have a "mission statement." I long ago decided that I wanted to write the kind of short stories I liked to read — the stuff of Flannery O'Connor, for instance; stuff that asked the Big Questions and ended up being anthologized in college texts because it lent itself to analysis. And I wanted to write stories and novels that weren't trendy and that, for that reason, might endure. "God's Will" is a good example: It wasn't of the fashion of the time; it wasn't a contemporary story.

When you have a mission statement, you're in a position to decide from whom you'll take your criticism — the good and the bad. Make sure it's someone you yourself respect. It's for this reason that I glow every time I remember that Ernest J. Gaines felt my stories "God's Will" and "Photographing Moscow" were "the best in the folder of finalists he received from the first readers" in the 1988 Deep South Writers Conference Contest. Gaines is the kind of writer that I would have wanted to get a compliment from, that I cared about getting a compliment from. Think about that the next time you're crushed when someone doesn't like your writing. Why do you care? Do you admire *their* writing? Do you wish you had written any of their work as I wish I'd written *The Autobiography of Miss Jane Pittman*?

MISSION STATEMENT

So, your last exercise is to take your mission statement and from it write your own manifesto. Here are a few quotations to help guide you. Each of them contains an implicit manifesto.

> In Cecilia's mind what she feels and the ability to write about it are not separate, and there has always been an interplay between her writing and her life, almost as if, in writing, she were checking on the progress of her own emotions regarding everything, (Lawrence Thornton, *Imagining Argentina*).

> We write to heighten our own awareness of life — we write to taste life twice, in the moment and in introspection. We write to be able to transcend our life, to reach beyond it, to teach ourselves to speak with others, to record the journey into the labyrinth, to expand our world, when we feel strangled, constricted, lonely. When I don't write I feel my world shrinking, I feel I lose my fire, my color, (*The Diary of Anais Nin*, Volume 5).

> The contemporary philosopher Richard Rorty — a prominent American liberal thinker — has written that the political role of the novelist in Western-style democratic societies is to develop fresh interpretations, to `redescribe.' He lists among the exemplars of this kind of writing George Orwell, who, in *1984*, redescribed for Western readers life under Communism — providing a terrible stark way of seeing, one that continues to have a profound influence, and not only in the West, (*The New York Times Magazine*, November 5, 1989).

> I spoke of the uselessness of art but added nothing truthful about its consolations. The solace of such work as I do with brain and heart lies in this — that only *there*, in the silences of the painter or the writer can reality be reordered, reworked and made to show its significant side. Our common actions in reality are simply the sackcloth covering which hides the cloth-of-gold — the meaning of the pattern. For us artists there waits the joyous compromise through art with all that wounded or defeated us in daily life; in this way, not to evade destiny, as the ordinary people try to do, but to fulfill it in its true potential — the imagination, (Lawrence Durrell, *Justine*,)

Always in Borges you are conscious of the `what if,' the playful relationship between the world of his stories and the one we live in, *(Lawrence Thornton,* Imagining Argentina*).*

If you can't learn from experience at least you can use it,(Martha Gellhorn, *Travels With Myself and Another*).

Kis is both a contemporary writer's writer and an ancient chronicler honoring vows made to the death — though readers who have cut their eyeteeth on the baby talk of much recent American fiction will find him nearly impossible to follow," (Charles Newman's review of Danito Kis' *Hourglass, The New York Times Magazine,* October 7, 1990).

That last really resonates with me. I love to come across a writer who believes in the intelligence of his or her reader — and they seem so few and far between these days. Part of the blame should sit squarely on the shoulders of those who've decided that "most people read at an xxx-grade level" and, therefore, everything should be written so that the "audience" understands. What nonsense! Even if most people read at, say, an eleventh-grade level, are they the audience for all books? And, besides, people rise to expectations — or lower themselves accordingly. One of the best examples of this I've ever seen was in the creative writing program from which I earned my master's. That program's head, Richard Stern, treated everyone in our group as if they were his fellow writers: We were compatriots struggling together. Because of this, we improved markedly in very short order.

When I wrote the following "Editor's Note" for the very first issue of my magazine, *Santa Fe Literary Review,* I now realize I was setting down my writing manifesto as well. Since I've extensively borrowed from my editor's note for this book — and since it contains much of this book's message and spirit — it's with this that I will end.

It's time for a return to a literature of meaning — stories and poems that we can sink our teeth into, food that fuels our thoughts and sparks our conversations into the stuff of which salons are made.

And that's what literature has always done: made us think, given us the opportunity to move beyond the narrow confines of our known world. We birth ourselves into new being with every piece of literature we read. But for some reason, this art's being allowed to die in this country. For too long now, we've seen works that attempt to duplicate what movies and television give us. This overlooks entirely the power of the written word. Unlike movies or TV, literature is a participatory art. We don't just watch like voyeurs peeping through the windows of strangers, we crawl through the window and live for a time in the world created by the author. We taste and touch and smell and hear and see and feel with our emotional bodies what it's like to be someone else. We walk for more than a mile in another's *moccasins — something that film, by its very nature, will never invite us to do.*

But what of contemporary stories — do they? So many of them seem to be academic exercises, perfectly crafted, but lacking the life found in the much-less-than-perfect stories of some of the masters of the art. Think of Ernest Hemingway's "A Clean, Well-Lighted Place." Who would publish it today? And yet, it's haunted many of us for years, like a dream we once had or a memory of an experience that sifts into consciousness in odd moments.

That, to me, is what makes a story good. Not that it's perfect, not even that it's skillfully rendered. No, sometimes those things get in the way of evoking what every writer must evoke in the reader: the dream. What makes a story good for me is that I can't quite shake it, it keeps coming back unbeckoned. It lives inside of me for months or years. Its images tangle into the web of my life so inextricably that, yes, they haunt me.

That's the basis on which I chose the stories and poems in this first issue: they all have haunted me for months or years. I'm happy, too, with these works because none is what I call "cookie cuttered," the stamp of too much that's written and published today. Herein you'll find variety: not one is like another; each bears the mark of the unique voice that brought it to life. With luck, you'll find a little eccentricity here, too, for as John Stuart Mill said in *On Liberty*:

> Eccentricity has always abounded when and where strength
> of character has abounded; and the amount of eccentricity

in a society has generally been proportional to the amount of genius, mental vigor; and moral courage which it contained. That so few now dare to be eccentric, marks the chief danger of our time.

Vive la différence!

THE CRITICS PAGE

WRITING EXERCISES

Some Books and Articles
Useful for the Fiction Author

Appelbaum, Judith, and Evans, Nancy. *How to Get Happily Published.*

Aristotle. *Poetics.*

Block, Lawrence. *Telling Lies for Fun and Profit.*

Bly, Carol. *The Passionate Accurate Story.*

Boggess, Louise. *How to Write Short Stories that Sell.*

Booth, Wayne. *The Rhetoric of Fiction.*

Bowker Company. *Literary Market Place.*

Brande, Dorothea. *Becoming a Writer.*

Brown, Rita Mae. *Starting from Scratch.*

Burack, Sylvia K. *The Writer's Handbook.*

Burnett, Hallie and Whit. *Fiction Writer's Handbook.*

Burroway, Janet. *Writing Fiction.*

Cameron, Julia. *The Artist's Way: A Spiritual Path to Higher Creativity.*

Campbell, Joseph. *The Hero With a Thousand Faces.*

Cappon, Rene J. *The Word.*

Cather, Willa. *Willa Cather on Writing.*

Charlton, James, and Mark, Lisbeth. *The Writer's Home Companion.*

Curtis, Richard. *How to Be Your Own Literary Agent.*

Dibell, Ansen. *Plot.*

Dickson, Frank A., and Smythe, Sandra, eds. *Handbook of Short Story Writing.*

Dillard, Annie. *Living by Fiction.*

Dillard, Annie. *The Writing Life.*

Egri, Lajos. *The Art of Dramatic Writing.*

Epel, Naomi. *Writers Dreaming.*

Field, Syd. *Screenplay: Foundations of Screenwriting.*

Field, Syd. *The Screenwriter's Workbook.*

Forster, E.M. *Aspects of the Novel.*

Gardner, John. *The Art of Fiction.*

Gardner, John. *On Becoming a Novelist.*

Gibson, William. *Shakespeare's Game.*

Goldberg, Natalie. *Writing Down the Bones.*

Heilbrun, Carolyn G. *Writing a Woman's Life.*

Henderson, Bill, ed. *The Publish-It-Yourself Handbook.*

Henderson, Bill, ed. *Rotten Reviews.*

Highsmith, Patricia. *Plotting and Writing Suspense Fiction.*

Hills, Rust. *Writing in General and the Short Story in Particular.*

Hollander, John. *Rhyme's Reason.*

Larsen, Michael. *Literary Agents: How to Get and Work with the Right one for You.*

Killien, Christi, and Bender, Sheila. *Writing in a Convertible with the Top Down.*

Kozak, Ellen M. *Every Writer's Guide to Copyright and Publishing Law.*

Kundera, Milan. *The Art of the Novel.*

Levoy, Greg. *This Business of Writing.*

Mamet, David. *Writing in Restaurants.*

May, Rollo. *The Courage to Create.*

Nolan, William F. *How to Write Horror Fiction.*

Ostriker, Alicia. *Writing Like a Woman.*

Perrine, Laurence. *Story and Structure.*

Polking, Kirk, and Meranus, Leonard S., eds. *Law and the Writer.*

Prose, Francine. "Writing Technique: Learning from Chekhov," in *Fiction Writer's Market '88*

Reid, Mildred I. *Writers: Let's Plot.*

Rockwell, F.A. *How to Write Plots that Sell.*

Scholes, Robert, and Klaus, Carl H. *Elements of Writing.*

Sternburg, Janet, ed. *The Writer on Her Work.*

Strickland, Bill, ed. *On Being a Writer.*

Strunk, William, Jr., and White, E.B. *The Elements of Style.*

Ueland, Brenda. *If You Want to Write.*

The University of Chicago Press. *The Chicago Manual of Style.*

Vogler, Christopher. *The Writer's Journey: Mythic Structure for Storytellers and Screenwriters.*

Williams, Joseph M. *Origins of the English Language.*

Williams, Joseph M. *Style: Ten Lessons in Clarity and Grace.*

Woolf, Virginia. *A Room of One's Own.*

INDEX

A

abyss 114
active incubation
　　3, 106, 108, 109, 110
active voice 81
Agony and the Ecstasy, The 42
analytical desperados 116
analytical mind
　　68, 97, 116, 118, 119
analytical process 108, 118
analytical thought
　　48, 107, 109, 110
anecdotes 25, 107
Aristotle 24, 70, 73, 75, 77, 121
armature 6, 46, 68, 72, 80, 115
Artist's Way, The 9
atmosphere 13, 67, 90, 91, 98
audience 3, 5, 24, 29, 30, 40, 94,
　　96, 97, 98, 122, 125

B

Barthelme's, Donald 84
Be It Ever So Humble 13
Beattie, Ann 94
Beattie, Ann 96
Becker, Carl 120
beginnings 9, 15, 59, 87, 91, 115
betes noires 98, 116
Billy Bathgate 79, 81, 97
birthing the story
　　3, 4, 102, 104, 108, 110, 115
bittersweet 34, 35, 38
Block, Lawrence 58
Böll, Heinrich 93, 94, 96
Borges, Jorge Luis 125
brain 2, 9, 27
Brande, Dorothea 111
Briggs, Jonathan 8
Brown, Rita Mae 84, 88, 98

building blocks, fiction's 2, 11, 12
building the pressure
　　106, 110, 111
bumping the reader 90, 118
Bundy, Ted 121
Butt-to-seat technique 112, 113

C

camera
　　3, 49, 87, 89, 90, 96, 97, 100
Cameron, Juila 9
Capote, Truman 99, 101
Carver, Raymond 82
cerebral cortex 27
characters
　　3, 5, 6, 8, 12, 13, 15, 24, 28,
29, 34, 40, 49, 52, 54, 56, 58,
67, 68, 69, 70, 71, 72, 74, 76,
77, 79, 81, 84, 89, 90, 91, 96, 99,
101, 108, 118, 121, 122, 127
Chekhov, Anton 29, 39
Christmas Memory, A 99
chronicling the movies in the mind
　　5, 7, 8, 23, 35, 38, 50, 67
clay digging, tips for 68
conscious mind 106, 108, 109
consciousness 11, 103, 119, 126
Continuum Trait
　　3, 70, 71, 72, 73, 74, 75, 76, 118
Courage to Create, The 5, 114
Craft of Fiction 1, 2, 4
creative process 42, 102
creativity 9, 104, 107, 108
critic, inner
　　2, 9, 10, 14, 21, 50, 116
critic, resident
　　118, 119, 120, 121, 123
criticicism 122, 123
critics 110, 116, 117, 123

Critics Page, The 2, 9
critique, rules of 116
critique, the art of 3, 116, 117, 118
Csikszentmihalyi, Mihaly 105

D

de Sade, Marquis 121
detailing it up 6, 14, 15
details
    14, 15, 16, 19, 20, 34, 35, 50,
54, 67, 69, 100, 101, 105, 110, 111
dialogue 49, 57
digging the clay
    3, 6, 15, 48, 51, 53, 55, 58, 67,
68, 69, 96, 97, 102
dilemma 3, 74, 75, 76, 77, 118
Doctorow, E.L. 79, 80, 81, 97
Dostoevsky, Fyodor 96, 122
dream, the fictional
    2, 5, 11, 12, 67, 100, 118, 126
Dream Warriors 69, 108
Durrell, Lawrence 20, 119, 124

E

emotions 110, 124
  and memory 27, 35
  evoking 24
  experiencing 24, 27
  using 34
empathy 14
end of the story 7, 118
epiphany 17
establishing shot 87, 88
evocative art 21
evoke
  emotions 24, 29, 34
  experience 18, 92
  images 16
  the dream 11, 15, 126

F

Faulkner, William 39, 82
fear 5, 6, 24, 27, 70, 105, 114

first person
    22, 83, 84, 85, 92, 93,
94, 95, 96, 97, 98, 99
Fleming, Dick 18
Flowering Judas 39, 103

G

Gaines, Ernest 123
Gardner, John 90
gestation 110
God's Will
    3, 41, 56, 57, 59, 84, 88, 89, 123
Goldberg, Natalie 47
Goldstein, Richard 114

H

hamartia 73
haunt, to 11, 39, 46, 67, 126
Hemingway, Ernest
    76, 82, 90, 104, 113, 126
Hills, Rust 117, 118
Hutton, James 73
Huxley, Aldous 105

I

Iliad 99
image or imaging
    11, 16, 26, 100, 101, 112
image seed 3, 39, 40, 41, 46, 67
image/emotion coin
    27, 30, 32, 34, 40
imager 120
images 2, 8, 11, 12, 13, 14, 21,
22, 25, 26, 27, 32, 39, 40, 41, 53,
82, 94, 100, 107, 119, 126
imaginative capacity 112
immersion activities
    3, 47, 104, 105, 106
incident 6, 39, 41, 67, 92, 109
incubation
    3, 102, 103, 104, 106, 108, 109, 111

J

journal 1, 35, 108, 109, 113, 120
Journal of a Solitude 111
joy writing 31, 32, 33
Joyce, James 17
Justine 119, 124

K

Kawabata, Yasunari 34
Kekulé von Stradonitz 107
Kollwitz, Kathe 28, 29, 30, 32
Krysl, Marilyn 41

L

La Chapelle, Mary 7, 8
L'Amour, Louis 113
Lawrence, D.H. 104
limbic system 2, 27
limited omniscient 89, 90
literary short story 83
Lorenz, Konrad 42

M

Mahfouz, Naguib 91, 96
manifesto 124, 125
May, Rollo 5, 114
McInerney, Jay 85, 86
meditation 105, 109, 112
memory
    11, 12, 27, 29, 31, 37, 38, 39,
    41, 46, 126
method acting 29
method writing
    30, 31, 35, 38, 40, 67
Mies van der Rohe, Ludwig 14
Mill, John Stuart 126
mission statement 123, 124
mnemonics 11, 46
moral voice 96
Morrell, David 101
movies in the mind
    2, 4, 5, 23, 27, 35, 38,
    67, 115, 120

N

naming 6
narrator 7, 84, 90, 96
nightly recap
    2, 19, 20, 23, 110, 111, 112
Nobel Prize for Literature
    34, 91, 93, 102, 123

O

O'Connor, Flannery 82
Oedipus Rex 72, 74
omniscient 89, 90, 96
On Liberty 126
Organick, Avrum 33

P

Painted Images 31
participatory art
    2, 29, 30, 32, 34, 38, 126
passive voice 81
past life 46
past tense 99, 120
Perchance to Dream
    21, 28, 35, 79, 120
Perrine, Laurence 91, 92
person
    first
        92, 93, 94, 95, 96, 97, 98, 99, 101
    second 96, 101
    third 96
perspective
    3, 91, 92, 94, 95, 97, 98, 101
perspective trials 3, 95, 97, 98
pity and fear 24, 70, 76
Poetics 24, 73
Poincaré, Henri 108, 109
point of view
    3, 91, 92, 93, 94, 121
Porter, Katherine Anne
    39, 41, 103
present participle 120, 123
present tense
    48, 95, 98, 99, 100, 101, 116, 117

pressure-cooker 106
Prose, Francine 39

R

revision 21, 31, 46
rhythm
7, 8, 19, 24, 25, 29, 30, 31, 34, 38, 67, 100, 108
Round Robin 2, 22, 23
Rule, Ann 121
rules of critique 116
Russell, Bertrand 102, 103, 106

S

Safire, William 82
Sagan, Mirium 47, 118
Salk, Jonas 106, 107
Santa Fe Literary Review 125
Sarton, May 104, 111
second person 83, 85, 86, 96, 101
senses 12, 14, 20
senses, inner 18
Sensory Repertoire 23
sensory repertoire 19
seventh sense 14
Shakespeare, William 29
silent movies 3, 110, 111
sing, making words
24, 34, 38, 83, 98, 121
sleeping on it 106
Solitude, A Return to the Self 9, 112
solitude, need for 111, 112
Sophocles 72, 73
Spencer, Herbert 102
split infinitives 120
Stanislavski, Constantin 29
Stern, Richard 125
Stevenson, Robert Louis 110
Stone, Irving 42
Storr, Anthony 9, 112
storyteller's voice
1, 2, 92, 93, 94, 96
storytelling tone 57
style 47, 81, 82, 83

suspense 24, 77
synaesthesia 20

T

technique
butt-to-seat 112, 113
continuum trait 3
imaging 11
meditative 112
method acting 29
participatory art 38
round robin 22
silent movie 3
timed writing 47, 48
writing 1, 2, 84, 92, 110
writing in restaurants 22
Teilhard de Chardin, Pierre 105
tense
48, 95, 98, 99, 100, 101, 116, 120
third person
22, 83, 84, 85, 90, 96
tip-of-the-iceberg thinking
6, 9, 30, 48, 109, 114
tips for clay digging 68
Tolstoy, Leo 90, 96
tone 49, 57, 67, 83, 89, 94
tragic flaw 74
Twain, Mark 92, 93

U

uncliché 21
unconscious, the
3, 6, 19, 35, 41, 46, 54, 55, 57, 89, 95, 102, 104, 106, 107, 108, 109, 110, 114

V

verb 81, 99, 120
vignette 42, 118
voice
active 81
at what distance 87, 94
definition 81, 82, 83

finding the
3, 6, 12, 16, 49, 79, 80, 81, 82,
83, 94, 95, 97, 106, 126
first person 84, 93
moral 96, 97
objective 90
passive 81
playing with 83
power of 98
second person 85
storyteller's 1, 92, 93, 94, 96

W

Wambaugh, Joseph 122
well, the
6, 7, 8, 9, 10, 21, 30, 31, 35,
41, 48, 54, 104, 109, 114
Welty, Eudora 15
Wilde, Oscar 21
Woolf, Virginia 111
Writing Down the Bones 47

Y

Yoko, Mori 13

OTHER FINE BOOKS FROM SHERMAN ASHER PUBLISHING

POEMS ALONG THE PATH, Judith Rafaela, ISBN: 0-9644196-0-2, $10.00, paperback, 48 pages. *Accessible poetry explores loves and losses, travels and faith, friends and family*

A PRESENCE OF ANGELS, Judyth Hill, ISBN: 0-9644196-1-0, $12.00, paperback, 72 pages. *Collected poems filled with the luminous presence of muses and angels, laughter and insight.*

WRITTEN WITH A SPOON, A POET'S COOKBOOK, Edited by Nancy Fay & Judith Rafaela, ISBN: 0-96441962-9, $18.00, paperback, 200 pages. *Food and verse on facing pages create this exciting collection of family recipes and original poems.*

MEN NEED SPACE, Judyth Hill, ISBN: 0-9644196-4-5, $12.00, paperback, 72 pages. *These poems, a tribute to growth in relationships and writing, move through expectation, disillusion, and disintegration, to seeing and loving people as they really are.*

LISTENING FOR CACTUS, Mary McGinnis, ISBN: 0-9644196-4-5, $14.00, paperback, 96 pages. *In this collection of poems we celebrate the seen and unseen, the disability experience, the New Mexico landscape, with its colors and silences. Blind since birth, McGinnis has written with power and humor about vision, wild pears, and the dreams she doesn't remember.* **Fall of 1996**

THE XY FILES, POEMS ON THE MALE EXPERIENCE, Edited by Fay & Rafaela, ISBN: 0-9644196-6-1, $18.00, 200 pages. *Illustrated with photos and line art, this collection shines the spotlight of poetic truth on the diversity and richness of the lives of men.* **Winter 1996**

ORDER TODAY!

Sherman Asher Publishing is an independent press dedicated to the rhythms of adventure. Our books are available at fine book stores or directly from the publisher at 1-800-474-1543.